OUT & ABOUT

IN THE WORLD OF COMPUTERS

An Introductory Computer Course for Beginning English Learners

COMPUTER BOOK

Amy Hemmert and Tina Sander

D1534388

Alta Book Center Publishers
www.altaesl.com

Acquisitions Editor: Aaron Almendares-Berman
Lead Content and Production Editor: Jamie Cross
Cover Design and Interior Illustrations: Andrew Lange Illustration
Interior Design and Page Layout: Wanda Espana/Wee Design Group

Acknowledgements

We would like to thank the following people for their help in producing this book:
Aaron Almendares-Berman and Simón Almendares-Berman for their leadership and vision.
Jamie Cross and Emily Wright for their editorial and design advice.
Andrew Lange for his creative artwork.
Wanda Espana for her outstanding design.
Rick Kappra for his original spark.
Marian Thacher for planting the seed that got us started.
The OTAN Technology Mentor Academy for all their support and input.
The many teachers who piloted our materials and provided us with invaluable feedback.
Our families for their support and encouragement.

Dedication

To all our students—past, present, and future—who never cease to amaze us, impress us, and motivate us and who bring so much energy and happiness to our lives.

Alta Book Center Publishers
www.altaesl.com

ISBN: 978-1-932383-04-1
Library of Congress Control Number: 2007922981

Contents

Scope and Sequence

English Content	Computer Skills		
	Microsoft Word	**Internet**	**Email**
Unit 1 In the Computer Room page 1			
• Vocabulary: classroom objects • Vocabulary: computer basics	• Using a mouse • Turning on a computer • Turning off a computer • Opening Microsoft Word • Closing Microsoft Word • Typing in Microsoft Word • Using a keyboard (Backspace, Space Bar, Enter)		
Unit 2 Nice to Meet You. page 13			
• Vocabulary: personal information	• Saving a Microsoft Word document • Opening a Microsoft Word document • Using a keyboard (moving the cursor, typing capital letters, typing a question mark) • Using the undo button and the redo button		
Unit 3 What Day Is Today? page 25			
• Vocabulary: everyday activities • Weekly schedules • Birthday calendars	• Inserting a memory stick or disk • Highlighting • Typing: bold • Typing: undo bold • Tables (vocabulary, inserting, and typing in) • Using print preview • Printing		

To the Teacher

Note: The complete teacher's guide is available as a free, downloadable pdf file at **www.outandabouteglish.com**.

OVERVIEW

Out and About in the World of Computers empowers beginning learners of English to succeed in the world of computers by developing their skills and confidence with Microsoft Word, the Internet, and email while simultaneously reinforcing their English skills.

COMPUTER REQUIREMENTS

Out and About in the World of Computers was designed for use with PCs equipped with Microsoft Windows, Microsoft Word, and Internet Explorer. For more details, visit **www.outandaboutenglish.com**.

OUTSTANDING FEATURES

- Ideal for teachers and students with little or no computer experience but easily adaptable for students with more computer knowledge.

- Addresses the needs of students enrolled in open-entry/open-exit programs.

- Teaches computer skills, English language learning content material, and vocabulary using picture-based, scaffolded activities in cohesive, theme-based units.

- Reinforces vocabulary and computer skills through innovative practice activities such as pairwork, class mingles, and real-life communication tasks.

- Builds student confidence through manageable assignments and end-of-unit checklists.

- Provides simple, yet engaging and realistic Microsoft Word and Internet activities that can be completed in less than one hour.

- Familiarizes students with Web conventions and prepares them to use Web sites by first exposing them to a simplified Web site, **www.outandaboutenglish.com**.

- Guides students through the process of signing up for an email account and introduces them to the basics of email use.

- Incorporates real-world portfolio projects for students to demonstrate their skills to teachers and future employers.

- Addresses potential computer issues.

- Fully integrates both the foundation skills and SCANS competencies.

COMPONENTS

Out and About in the World of Computers is made up of three components: the Computer Book, the Teacher's Guide, and the Web site.

Computer Book Designed as a student workbook, the Computer Book starts with the basics of computers and Microsoft Word and gradually progresses to cover the more advanced features of Microsoft Word, the Internet, and email. The Computer Book is effective as a stand-alone text or as a complement to the *Out and About* Student Book (or another beginning-level English textbook).

The Computer Book consists of thirteen units, each focusing on a specific theme or set of themes related to everyday life and mirroring those found in the *Out and About* Student Book. Each unit introduces new computer skills but also reviews material from previous units. Most units also include at least one student-generated project that can be printed and taken home. Included in the Computer Book are pairwork activities, interviews, class mingles, information-gap activities, matching tasks, and much more. The highly interactive Computer Book builds English proficiency and develops computer skills while addressing a range of learning styles.

Teacher's Guide The Teacher's Guide is available as a free, downloadable pdf file at **www.outandaboutenglish.com**.

The Computer Book is supported by the user-friendly Teacher's Guide. The Teacher's Guide provides unit objectives, unit outlines, and lists of key vocabulary to allow for easy and thorough class preparation. The suggested, easy-to-follow procedures are stated in a clear step-by-step format. The Teacher's Guide also offers additional activities and adaptations for more advanced computer users, and it provides the teacher with relevant computer-related background information and Web sites.

Web Site The *Out and About in the World of Computers* Web site, **www.outandaboutenglish.com**, prepares students to navigate the Web. It familiarizes them with the most common uses of the Internet through interactive activities involving job listings, housing ads, virtual bus schedules, movie guides, restaurant menus, and more. The vocabulary used on the site is appropriate for beginning language learners, and the uncluttered site design is both appealing and easy to navigate.

SUGGESTIONS FOR CLASSROOM USE

Note: See the downloadable Teacher's Guide at www.outandaboutenglish.com for more instruction.

Vocabulary Vocabulary can be presented to the whole class by using an overhead projector or instructing students to look in their books. Elicit as much information as you can from the students, using different strategies and relying on realia whenever possible. Do not hesitate to try different strategies, such as making drawings on the board, using gestures, and supplementing with pictures and photographs.

Mingles Mingles are designed to provide focused speaking practice with a large number of people. They are repetitive in nature and involve the skills of reading, writing, listening, and speaking. The classroom is generally noisy at this time, so students are less self-conscious about speaking English. Stop the activity when students have finished their worksheets or when you feel that they have received enough practice.

Partners If possible, try to pair students from different language backgrounds. If you have an odd number of students, you will have to ask some students to form a group of three. You may want to choose three students who you think will complete the activity rather quickly so that they will finish at roughly the same time as the other students. Alternatively, you can choose to work with the extra student, if you feel that you will not need to circulate among the other students. If you have new students entering the class on a regular basis you may want to pair them with more advanced students who can bring them up to speed. Alternatively, you may designate alternating helpers to assist new students.

Groupwork Depending on the makeup of your class, you may want to form new groups for each activity. This will allow students of different language backgrounds, proficiency levels, ages, and genders to work together.

Portfolio Portfolio activities are tangible, student-generated products designed to instill pride, confidence, and a sense of accomplishment. These real-life projects demonstrate student progress and tie together the skills and concepts students have learned. These projects are multilevel in nature, supporting beginning-level students while providing opportunities to challenge more advanced students.

The quality of the portfolio items will vary depending on the proficiency and confidence of the student. Some beginning students will merely complete these projects. The more advanced computer users should be shown how to embellish their projects by taking advantage of more sophisticated features that are explained in the Teacher's Guide. Feel free to pick and choose the projects most relevant to your students' needs.

SCANS COMPETENCIES

The Secretary's Commission on Achieving Necessary Skills was established by the Department of Labor in 1990. In 1991, the commission released its first report, *What Work Requires of Schools—SCANS Report for America 2000*, which identifies three foundation skills and five competencies that are required in order to be successful in the workplace. The foundation skills include basic skills (reading, writing, listening, speaking, and math); thinking skills (creative thinking, decision-making, problem solving and reasoning); and personal qualities (responsibility, self-esteem, social skills, self-management, and integrity). The competencies list desirable workplace qualities: working well with others, teamwork, acquiring and evaluating data, understanding systems, and using technology.

Out and About in the World of Computers has fully integrated both the foundation skills and SCANS competencies throughout the book. Activities are designed to develop the learners' interpersonal skills, responsibility, self-esteem, learning strategies, and self-management, while strengthening language, critical thinking, and technology skills.

In the Computer Room

1.1 Vocabulary

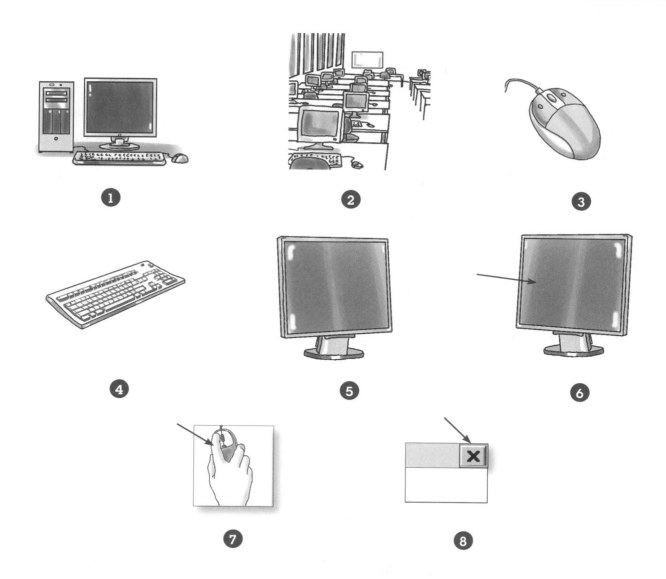

①

②

③

④

⑤

⑥

⑦

⑧

1.2 Speaking

PARTNER A: *Look at page 1.*

PARTNER B: *Look at page 2. Say the words.*

PARTNER A: *Point to the picture.*

Change roles and repeat.

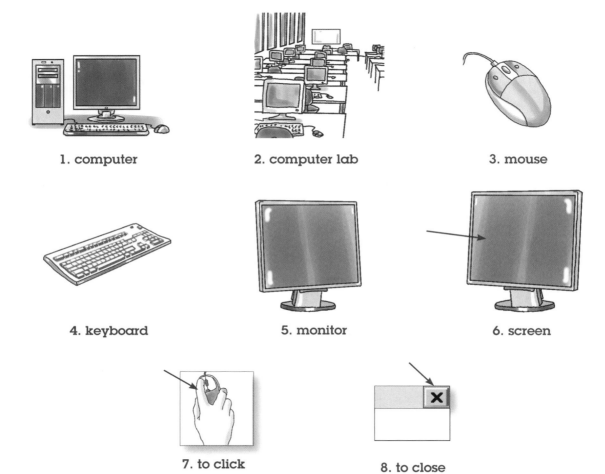

1. computer   2. computer lab   3. mouse

4. keyboard   5. monitor   6. screen

7. to click   8. to close

1.3 Writing

Listen to your teacher. Write the words. Show your partner.

1. _Computer_   5. _monitor_

2. _Computer lab_   6. _screen_

3. _mouse_   7. _to click_

4. _keyboard_   8. _to close_

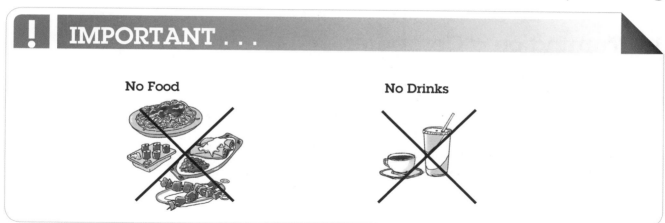

No Food

No Drinks

1.4 Using a Mouse

1. Look at your teacher. Hold the mouse.

 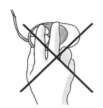   

2. Look at your teacher. Left click the mouse.

left **middle** **right**

3. Look at your teacher. Double-click the mouse.

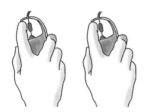

Click. Click.

4. Show your partner. Is it OK?

1.5 Turning on a Computer

1. Turn on the computer.

2. Turn on the monitor.

3. Wait.

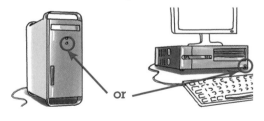

or

**Press
the button.**

← **Press
the button.**

1.6 Turning off a Computer

1. Click:

2. Click:

3. Click:

Practice

1. Turn on the computer.

2. Turn off the computer.

3. Repeat three times.

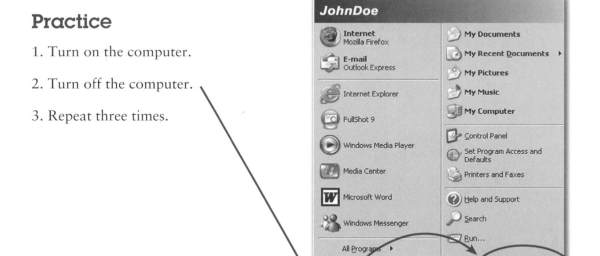

Note to the Teacher: Some networks require logging on and logging off. See the online teacher's guide at www.outandaboutenglish.com for more information.

1.7 The Computer Screen

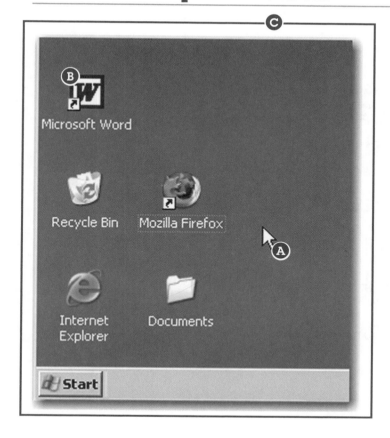

Match A, B, C.

1. _____ desktop

2. _____ icon

3. _____ pointer

Practice

Listen to your teacher. Write the words. Show your partner.

1. _____

2. _____

3. _____

1.8 Opening and Closing Microsoft Word

Opening Microsoft Word

To open, double-click 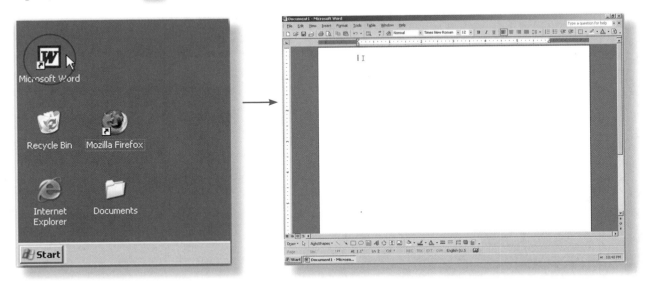.

Closing Microsoft Word

To close, click ☒.

Practice

1. Turn on the computer.

2. Open Microsoft Word 🆆.

3. Close Microsoft Word ☒.

4. Repeat steps 2 and 3.

1.9 Typing in Microsoft Word

1. Open Microsoft Word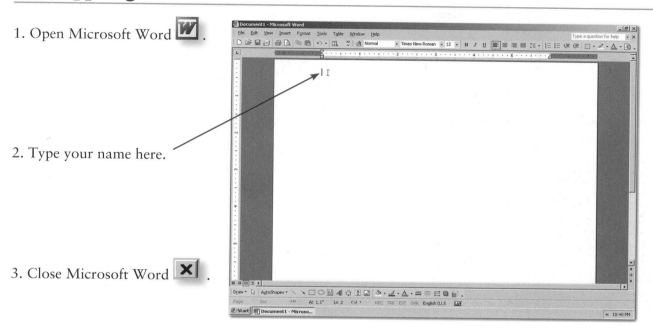

2. Type your name here.

3. Close Microsoft Word

4. Click **No**.

Note to the Teacher: Saving has intentionally NOT been introduced until Unit 2.
See the online teacher's guide at www.outandaboutenglish.com for more information.

1.10 Using a Keyboard

Press **Backspace** to erase.

Press the **Space Bar** between words.

Press **Enter** for a new line.

1. Open Microsoft Word 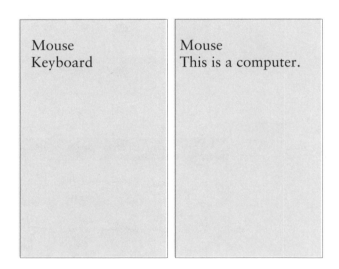 .

2. Type **mouse.**

3. Press **Enter.**

4. Type **keyboard.**

5. Erase **keyboard.**

6. Type **This is a computer.**

7. Close Microsoft Word ⊠ .

Mouse Keyboard	Mouse This is a computer.

Practice

1. Open Microsoft Word ⊞ .

2. Type these words:

| book | write | read | look | repeat | listen |

3. Close Microsoft Word ⊠ .

Note to the Teacher: This is not intended to be a typing lesson. See the online teacher's guide at www.outandaboutenglish.com for more information.

1.11 Review

Before You Start

Listen to your teacher. Write the words. Show your partner.

1. _____
2. _____
3. _____

4. _____
5. _____
6. _____

Typing

1. Open Microsoft Word  .

2. Type the words.

3. Close Microsoft Word .

Before You Start

Look around the classroom. What do you see? Write the words. Show your partner.

1. _____
2. _____
3. _____
4. _____

5. _____
6. _____
7. _____
8. _____

Typing

1. Open Microsoft Word .

2. Type the words.

3. Close Microsoft Word .

1.12 Homework

Typing

Look around your home. What do you see? Write eight words:

My Home

1. _____   5. _____

2. _____   6. _____

3. _____   7. _____

4. _____   8. _____

1. Open Microsoft Word  .

2. Type the words.

3. Close Microsoft Word .

Unit 1 End-of-Unit Checklist

Unit 1		
I can . . .		
. . . use a mouse.	☐ Yes!	☐ Not yet.
. . . click a mouse.	☐ Yes!	☐ Not yet.
. . . double-click a mouse.	☐ Yes!	☐ Not yet.
. . . turn on a computer.	☐ Yes!	☐ Not yet.
. . . turn off a computer.	☐ Yes!	☐ Not yet.
. . . open Microsoft Word.	☐ Yes!	☐ Not yet.
. . . close Microsoft Word.	☐ Yes!	☐ Not yet.
. . . type in Microsoft Word.	☐ Yes!	☐ Not yet.
. . . use a keyboard.	☐ Yes!	☐ Not yet.
. . . press Backspace to erase.	☐ Yes!	☐ Not yet.
. . . press the Space Bar between words.	☐ Yes!	☐ Not yet.
. . . press Enter for a new line.	☐ Yes!	☐ Not yet.

Nice to Meet You.

2.1 Vocabulary

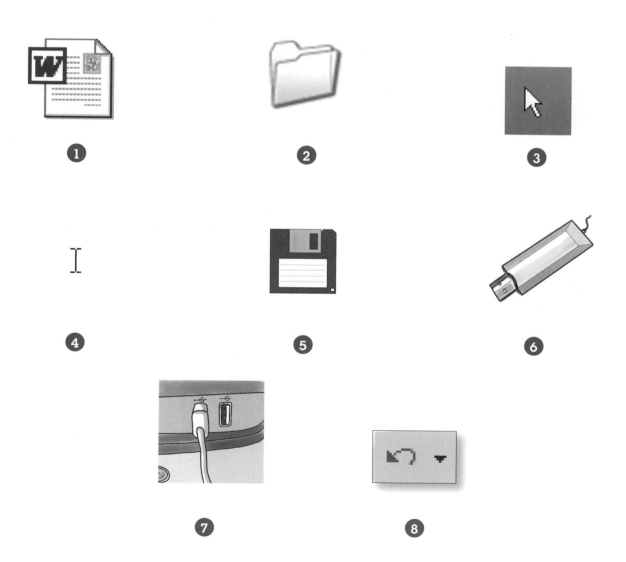

2.2 Speaking

PARTNER A: *Look at page 13.*

PARTNER B: *Look at page 14. Say the words.*

PARTNER A: *Point to the picture.*

Change roles and repeat.

1. document

2. folder

3. pointer

4. cursor

5. disk

6. memory stick

7. USB port

8. to undo

2.3 Writing

Listen to your teacher. Write the words. Show your partner.

1. _____

2. _____

3. _____

4. _____

5. _____

6. _____

7. _____

8. _____

Note to the Teacher: There are multiple names for the item "memory stick."
See the online teacher's guide at www.outandaboutenglish.com for more information.

> **! IMPORTANT . . .**
>
> **Inserting a Memory Stick . . .**
>
> - Hold the memory stick.
> - Insert the memory stick into the USB port.
>
> **Inserting a Disk . . .**
>
> - Hold the disk with the label up.
> - Insert the disk.

2.4 Review

Turning on a computer

1. Turn on the computer.

2. Turn on the monitor.

3. Wait.

Turning off a computer

1. Click **Start**.

2. Click **Turn Off Computer**.

3. Click **Turn Off**.

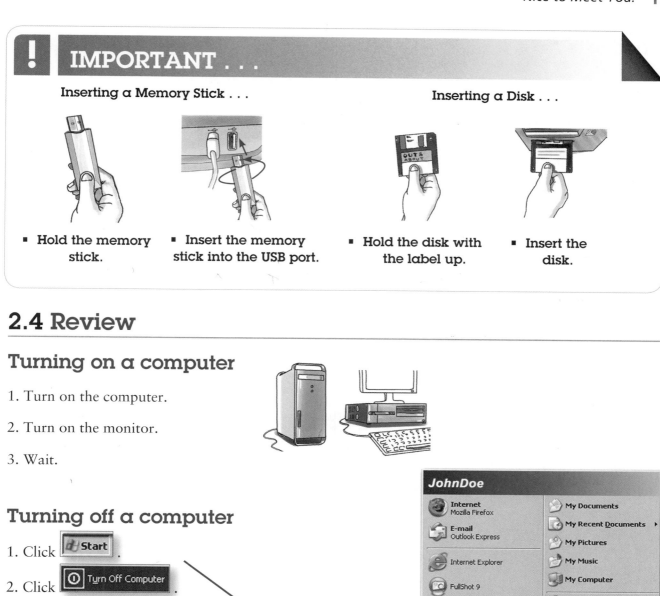

Opening and Closing Microsoft Word

1. Turn on the computer.

2. Double-click **W**.

3. Click **×**.

4. Turn off the computer.

Practice

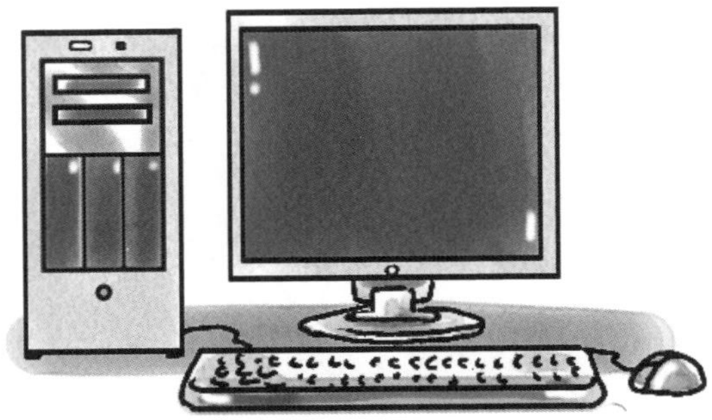

1. Turn on the computer.
2. Open Microsoft Word.
3. Type your name.
4. Close Microsoft Word.
5. Turn off the computer.
6. Repeat steps 1–4.

2.5 Saving a Microsoft Word Document

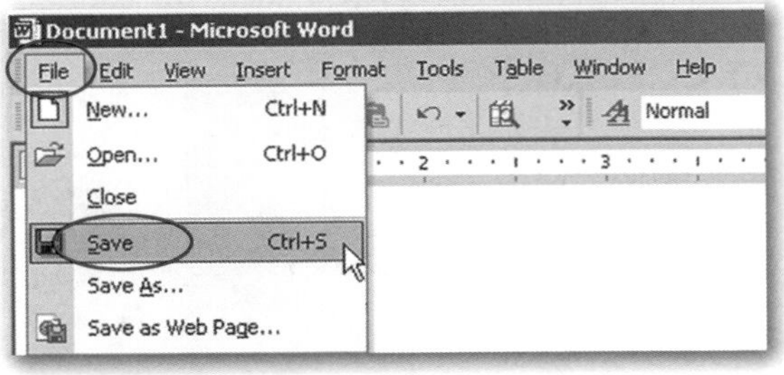

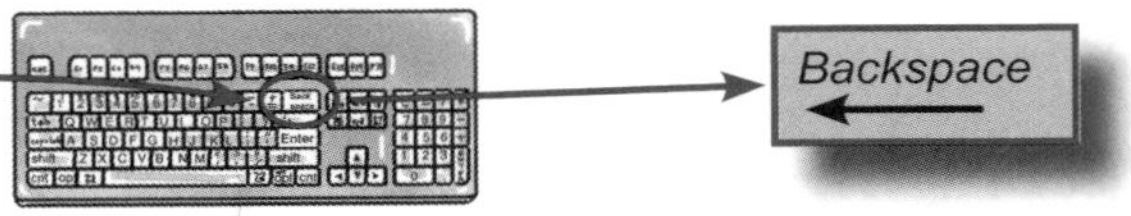

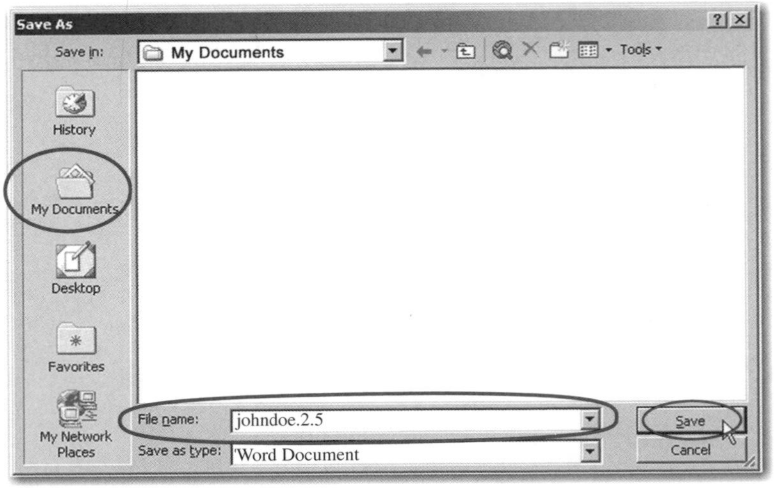

1. Open Microsoft Word.
2. Click **File.**
3. Click **Save**.
4. Click **My Documents.**
5. Click in the **File name** box.
6. Erase **Document1.**
7. Type **yourname.2.5.**
8. Click **Save**.
9. Type these words:

Screen
Desktop
Icon
Pointer

10. Click File.
11. Click **Save**.
12. Close Microsoft Word.

Note to the Teacher: "Yourname" is intended to be the student's name. All examples in this book use the name "John Doe." See the online teacher's guide at www.outandaboutenglish.com for more information.

Practice 1

1. Open Microsoft Word  .

2. Save the document as **yourname.2.5.practice** .

- Click **File**.
- Click **Save** .
- Click **My Documents**.
- In the box, type **yourname.2.5.practice**.
- Click **Save** .

3. Type these words:

Document
Folder
Disk
Memory stick

4. Save:

- Click **File**.
- Click **Save** .

5. Close Microsoft Word .

Practice 2

1. Open Microsoft Word .

2. Save the document as **yourname.2.5.words** .

3. Type these words:

Keyboard
Monitor
Computer

4. Save .

5. Close Microsoft Word .

2.6 Opening a Microsoft Word Document

1. Open Microsoft Word [W].

2. Click **File**.

3. Click **Open** [⬆].

4. Click **My Documents**.

5. Click **yourname.2.5**.

6. Click **Open**.

7. Close Microsoft Word [X].

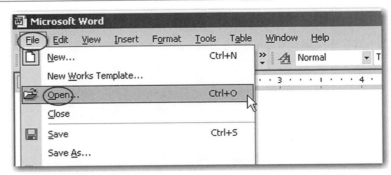

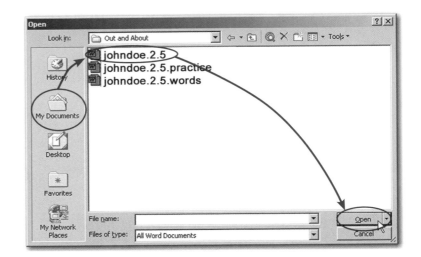

Practice

1. Open Microsoft Word [W].

2. Open your document:

   - Click **File**.
   - Click **Open** [⬆].
   - Click **My Documents**.
   - Click **yourname.2.5**.
   - Click **Open**.

3. Close Microsoft Word [X].

4. Open Microsoft Word [W].

5. Open **yourname.2.5.practice**.

6. Close Microsoft Word [X].

7. Repeat steps 1–5 to
   open **yourname.2.5.words**.

2.7 Using a Keyboard

1. Open Microsoft Word .

2. Open the document **yourname.2.5.practice.**

Moving the Cursor in a Document

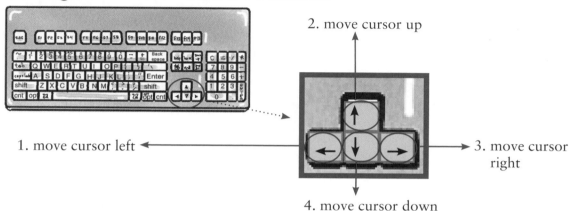

2. move cursor up

1. move cursor left

3. move cursor right

4. move cursor down

Typing Capital Letters

ABCDEFGHIJKLMNOPQRSTUVWXYZ

1. Hold down one of the **Shift** keys.

   shift

2. Press a letter.

   M

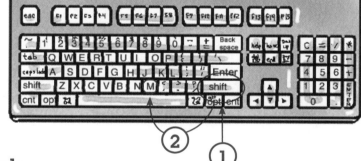

Typing a Question Mark

3. Hold down one of the **Shift** keys.

   shift

4. Press ?.

   ?

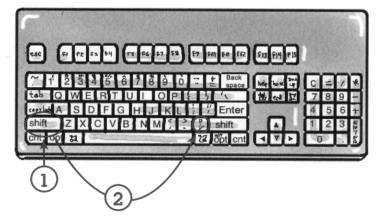

5. Close Microsoft Word .

2.8 Typing: My Information

1. Open Microsoft Word 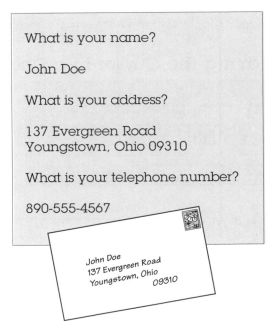 .

2. Save the document as **yourname.2.8.information** .

3. Type **What is your name?**

4. Type your name.

5. Type **What is your address?**

6. Type your address.

7. Type **What is your telephone number?**

8. Type your telephone number.

9. Save .

10. Close Microsoft Word .

Example:

What is your name?

John Doe

What is your address?

137 Evergreen Road
Youngstown, Ohio 09310

What is your telephone number?

890-555-4567

John Doe
137 Evergreen Road
Youngstown, Ohio   09310

2.9 Using the Undo Button and the Redo Button

1. Open Microsoft Word .

2. Open **yourname.2.8.information** .

3. Type **What language do you speak?**

4. Erase **What language do you speak?**

5. Click the Undo button .

6. Click the Redo button .

7. Press **Enter.**

8. Type a language you speak.

9. Press **Enter.**

10. Save .

11. Close Microsoft Word .

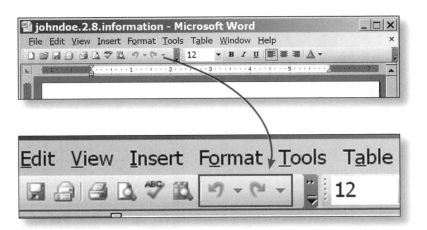

2.10 Typing: My Partner's Information

1. Open Microsoft Word  .

2. Save the document as **yourname.2.10.mypatrner** .

3. Type these questions:

> What is your first name?
> Where are you from?
> What is your telephone number?
> What is your address?

4. Work with a partner:

    Partner A: Ask the questions.
    Partner B: Answer the questions.
    Partner A: Type the answers.

5. Save .

6. Close Microsoft Word .

2.11 Typing: Vocabulary

Before You Start

Listen to your teacher. Write the words. Show your partner.

1. _____   5. _____

2. _____   6. _____

3. _____   7. _____

4. _____   8. _____

Typing

1. Open Microsoft Word .

2. Save the document as
   yourname.2.11.vocabulary .

3. Type the words.

4. Save .

5. Close Microsoft Word .

2.12 Typing: Classroom Interviews

Before You Start

Talk to two classmates.

Ask the questions. Write the answers:

	Classmate 1	Classmate 2
What's your first name?		
What's your last name?		
What country are you from?		
What languages do you speak?		
What's your nationality?		
What city do you live in?		

Classroom Interviews

1. Open Microsoft Word .

2. Save the document as **yourname.2.12.interview** .

3. Type the questions and answers.

4. Save .

5. Close Microsoft Word .

Example:

What's your first name?

Carlos

What's your last name?

Irizari

2.13 Homework

A Document: My Friends

1. Talk to two friends.

2. Ask the questions. Write the answers:

	Friend 1	Friend 2
What's your first name?		
What's your last name?		
What country are you from?		
What languages do you speak?		
What's your nationality?		
What's your street address?		
What city do you live in?		
What state/province or country do you live in?		
What's your zip code?		
What's your telephone number?		

3. Open Microsoft Word W .

4. Save the document as **yourname.2.13.friends** 💾 .

5. Type the questions and answers.

6. Save 💾 .

7. Close Microsoft Word X .

Ciao!

Example:

What's your first name?

Arnaud

Unit 2 End-of-Unit Checklist

REVIEW		
I can . . .		
. . . use a mouse.	☐ Yes!	☐ Not yet.
. . . turn on a computer.	☐ Yes!	☐ Not yet.
. . . turn off a computer.	☐ Yes!	☐ Not yet.
. . . open Microsoft Word.	☐ Yes!	☐ Not yet.
. . . close Microsoft Word.	☐ Yes!	☐ Not yet.
. . . use a keyboard.	☐ Yes!	☐ Not yet.
. . . erase words in Microsoft Word.	☐ Yes!	☐ Not yet.
UNIT 2		
I can . . .		
. . . save Microsoft Word documents.	☐ Yes!	☐ Not yet.
. . . open Microsoft Word documents.	☐ Yes!	☐ Not yet.
. . . move the cursor in Microsoft Word documents.	☐ Yes!	☐ Not yet.
. . . type capital letters.	☐ Yes!	☐ Not yet.
. . . use the Undo button.	☐ Yes!	☐ Not yet.
. . . use the Redo button.	☐ Yes!	☐ Not yet.

What Day Is Today?

3.1 Vocabulary

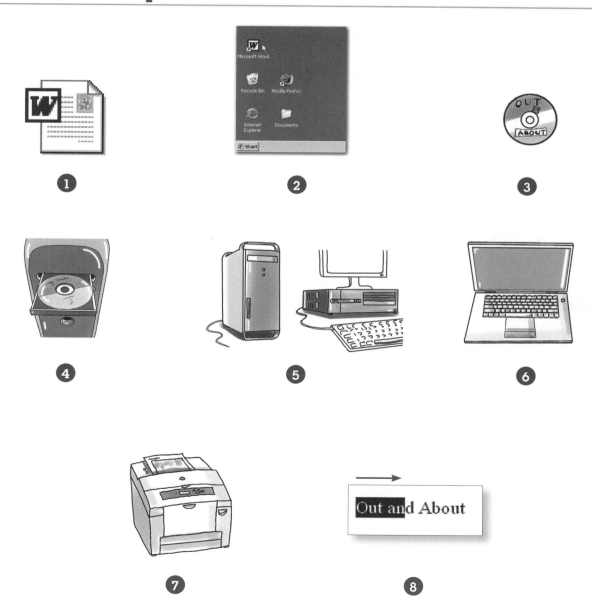

3.2 Speaking

PARTNER A: *Look at page 25.*

PARTNER B: *Look at page 26. Say the words.*

PARTNER A: *Point to the picture.*

Change roles and repeat.

1. document   2. desktop   3. CD   4. CD drive

5. desktop computer   6. laptop computer   7. printer   8. to highlight

3.3 Writing

Listen to your teacher. Write the words. Show your partner.

1. _____   5. _____

2. _____   6. _____

3. _____   7. _____

4. _____   8. _____

IMPORTANT . . .

Inserting a CD . . .

- **Push the button to open the tray.**
- **Place the CD in the tray.**
- **Push the button to close.**

3.4 Review

Saving a Microsoft Word Document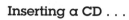

1. Open Microsoft Word .

2. Save the document as **yourname.3.4.review:**

- Click **File.**
- Click **Save** .
- Click **My Documents.**
- Type **yourname.3.4.review** in the **File name** box.
- Click **Save** .

3. Close Microsoft Word .

Opening a Microsoft Word Document

1. Open Microsoft Word .

2. Open **yourname.3.4.review:**

- Click **File.**
- Click **Open** .
- Click **My Documents.**
- Click **yourname.3.4.review.**
- Click **Open.**

3. Type the words from **activity 3.2.**

Using Undo and Redo

4. Click the Undo button .

5. Click the Redo button .

6. Save .

7. Close Microsoft Word .

3.5 Typing: Highlighting

1. Open Microsoft Word .

2. Open **yourname.3.4.review.**

3. Highlight **Document::**

   - Click before the word.
   - Hold down and move to the end.
   - Let go.

4. Press delete .

5. Click the Undo button .

6. Highlight all of the words:

   - Click before the first word.
   - Hold down and move to the end of the last word.
   - Let go.

7. Press delete .

8. Click the Undo button .

9. Save .

10. Close Microsoft Word .

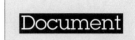

3.6 Typing: Bold

1. Open **Microsoft Word** .

2. Open **yourname.3.4.review** 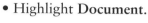.

3. Make the word **Document** bold: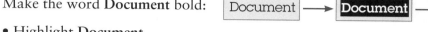

   - Highlight **Document**.

   - Click 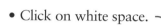.

   - Click on white space.

4. Make **Laptop computer** bold:

   - Highlight
     Laptop computer.

   - Click **B**.

   - Click on white space.

5. Save 💾.

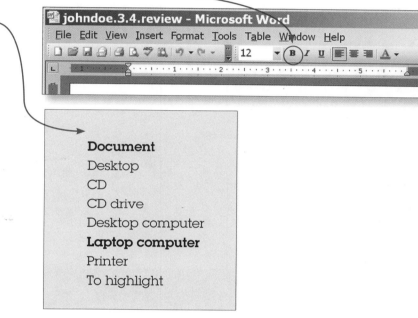

3.7 Typing: Undo Bold

1. Continue working in the document **yourname.3.4.review.**

2. Highlight **Laptop computer**.

3. Click **B**.

4. Click on white space.

5. Save 💾.

6. Close Microsoft Word ❎.

3.8 Tables: Vocabulary

Vocabulary 1

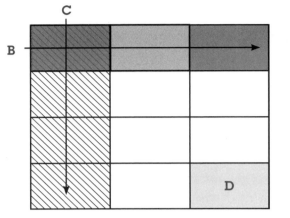

Match and write the letters.

1. ___A___ table

2. _____ cell

3. _____ row

4. _____ column

Vocabulary 2

Match and write the letters.

1. ___C___ 1 row, 2 columns

2. _____ 3 rows, 2 columns

3. _____ 1 row, 1 column

4. _____ 3 rows, 1 column

Practice

Listen to your teacher. Write the words. Show your partner.

1. _____

2. _____

3. _____

4. _____

3.9 Tables

Inserting Tables

1. Open Microsoft Word 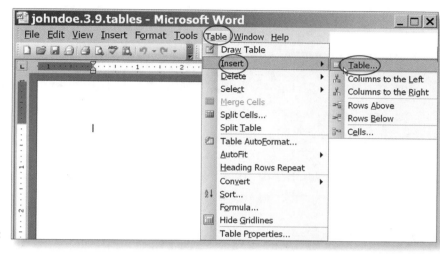.

2. Save the document as **yourname.3.9.tables** .

3. Click **Table**.

4. Click **Insert**.

5. Click **Table**.

6. Change the **Number of columns**:
   - Click in the box.
   - Press **Backspace**.
   - Type **2**.

7. Change the **Number of rows**:
   - Click in the box.
   - Press **Backspace**.
   - Type **4**.

8. Click **OK**.

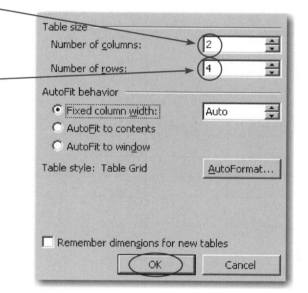

Typing Inside Tables

1. Click in the cell.

2. Type one.

3. Click in the cell.

4. Type two.

one	two
	three

5. Click in the cell.

6. Type three.

7. Save .

8. Close Microsoft Word .

3.10 My Portfolio: My Weekly Schedule

1. Open Microsoft Word .

2. Save the document as **yourname.3.10.schedule** 💾.

3. Insert a table with eight columns and four rows. It will look like this:

   - Click **Table**.
   - Click **Insert**.
   - Click **Table**.
   - Type **8** for Number of columns.
   - Type **4** for Number of rows.
   - Click **OK**.

4. Type the days of the week in the first row.

5. Make the days of the week bold:

   - Highlight the row.
   - Click **B**.

Example:

	Sunday	Monday	Tuesday	Wednesday	Thursday	Friday	Saturday

6. Type three times during the day in the first column.

7. Make the times bold:

   - Highlight the column.
   - Click **B**.

8. Type your daily activities in the other cells.

Example:

	Sunday	Monday	Tuesday	Wednesday	Thursday	Friday	Saturday
8:00	Housework	School		School		School	
12:00			Study			Relax	Exercise
6:15		Work		Sleep			

9. Save 💾.

10. Close Microsoft Word ❎.

3.11 Using Print Preview

1. Open Microsoft Word 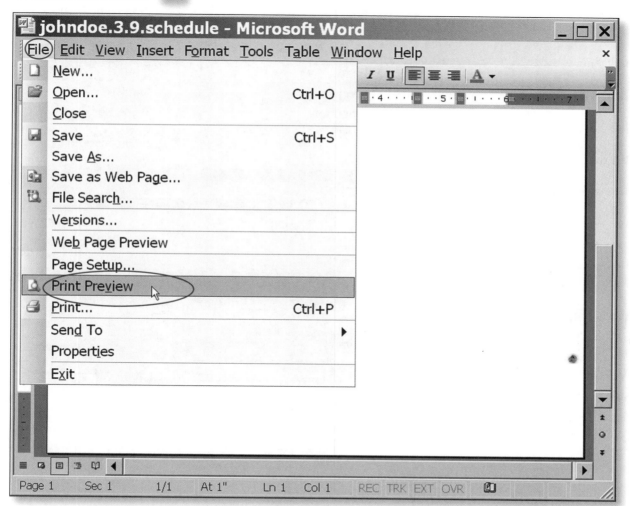.

2. Open **yourname.3.10.schedule** .

3. Read your document. Change one of your daily activities.

4. Save .

5. Click **File**.

6. Click **Print Preview** .

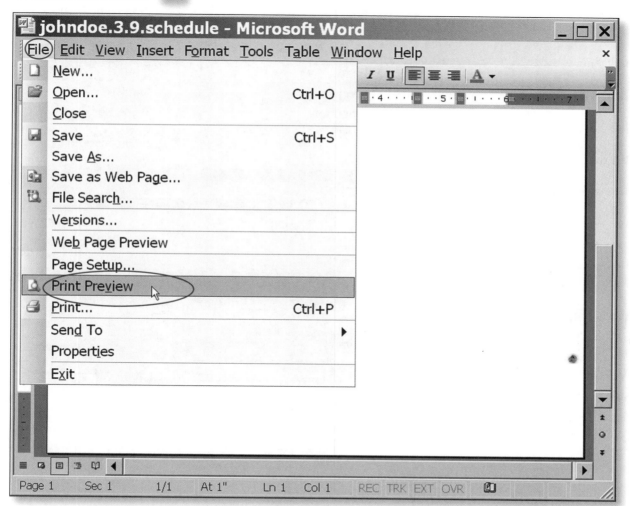

7. Look. Is the document OK?

8. Click **Close**.

9. Close Microsoft Word .

3.12 Printing

1. Open Microsoft Word 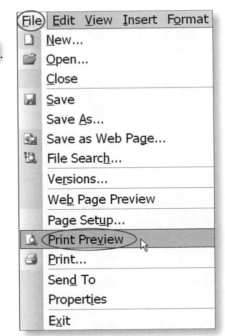.

2. Open **yourname.3.10.schedule** .

3. Ask your teacher, "May I print?"

4. Click **File.**

5. Click **Print Preview.**

6. Look. Is the document OK?

7. Click **Close.**

8. Click **File.**

9. Click **Print** .

10. Click **OK.**

11. Add this page to your portfolio.

12. Close **Microsoft Word** .

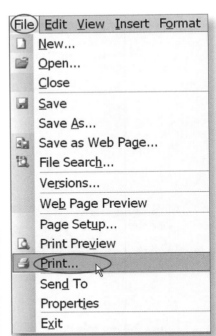

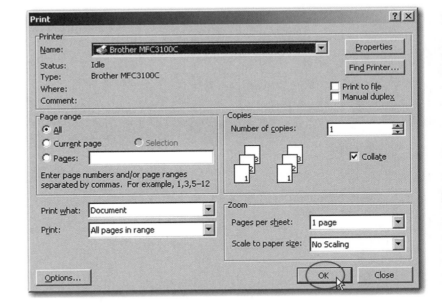

3.13 My Portfolio: A Birthday Calendar

Before You Start

Ask ten classmates about their birthdays:

A: *When's your birthday?*
B: *My birthday is November 16ᵗʰ. When's your birthday?*
A: *My birthday is January 10ᵗʰ.*

Write their names and birthdays:

Name	Birthday

A Birthday Calendar

1. Open Microsoft Word .

2. Save the document as **yourname.3.13.birthdaycalendar** .

3. Make a table with three columns and eight rows.

4. Type the months of the year.

5. Type the names and birthdays from page 35.

6. Type the holidays.

7. Bold the months.

8. Save .

9. Click **File**.

10. Click **Print Preview**.

11. Look. Is the document OK?

12. Click **Close**.

13. Click **File**.

14. Click **Print** .

15. Add this page to your portfolio.

16. Close Microsoft Word .

Example:

January	February	March
12 Robert	2 Mohammed	14 Amy
April	**May**	**June**
July	**August**	**September**
13 Grace		
October	**November**	**December**
25 Huang		25 Christmas 26 Paul

3.14 Homework

Inserting Tables: A Friend's Schedule

1. Talk to a friend.

2. Ask the questions and write the answers:

My Friend's Schedule

What do you do on Mondays at 10:00? _____

What do you do on Tuesdays at 12:00? _____

What do you do on Wednesdays at 4:00? _____

What do you do on Fridays at 5:00? _____

---

3. Open Microsoft Word ⬜.

4. Save the document as **yourname.3.14.friendsschedule** 💾.

5. Insert a table with eight columns and five rows.

6. Type the days of the week in the first row.

7. Type the times in the first column.

8. Type your friend's activities in the other cells.

9. Save 💾.

10. Print the table 🖨.

11. Give the weekly schedule to your friend.

12. Close Microsoft Word ❌.

Unit 3 End-of-Unit Checklist

REVIEW		
I can . . .		
. . . open Microsoft Word.	☐ Yes!	☐ Not yet.
. . . close Microsoft Word.	☐ Yes!	☐ Not yet.
. . . save Microsoft Word documents.	☐ Yes!	☐ Not yet.
. . . open Microsoft Word documents.	☐ Yes!	☐ Not yet.
. . . use the Undo and Redo buttons.	☐ Yes!	☐ Not yet.
UNIT 3		
I can . . .		
. . . highlight words.	☐ Yes!	☐ Not yet.
. . . use bold.	☐ Yes!	☐ Not yet.
. . . undo bold.	☐ Yes!	☐ Not yet.
. . . insert tables.	☐ Yes!	☐ Not yet.
. . . type inside tables.	☐ Yes!	☐ Not yet.
. . . use print preview.	☐ Yes!	☐ Not yet.
. . . print.	☐ Yes!	☐ Not yet.

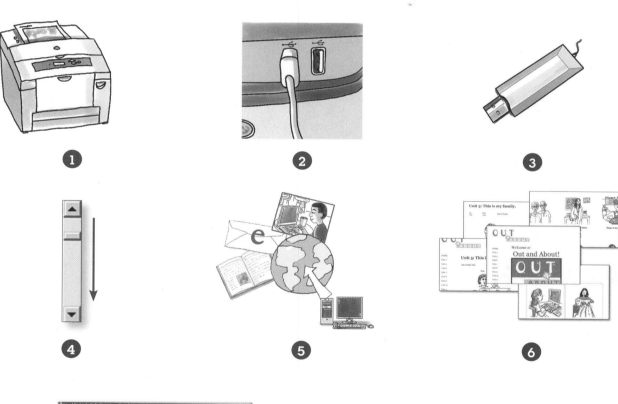

UNIT 4

What Do You Do?

4.1 Vocabulary

1

2

3

4

5

6

http://www.outandaboutenglish.com

7

8

4.2 Speaking

PARTNER **A:** *Look at page 39.*

PARTNER **B:** *Look at page 40. Say the words.*

PARTNER **A:** *Point to the picture.*

Change roles and repeat.

1. printer

2. USB port

3. memory stick

4. to scroll *bar*

5. the Internet

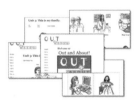

6. Web site

7. Web page

http://www.outandaboutenglish.com

8. Web address

URL

4.3 Writing

Listen to your teacher. Write the words. Show your partner.

1. _____

2. _____

3. _____

4. _____

5. _____

6. _____

7. _____

8. _____

! IMPORTANT . . .

You must put the pointer (arrow) on the button.

4.4 Review

Before You Start

Write each word in the correct column below:

screen	doctor	keyboard	carpenter
mechanic	icon	dishwasher	cashier
mouse	homemaker	pointer	disk

Jobs	Computer Words

Inserting a Table

1. Open Microsoft Word .

2. Save the document as **yourname.4.4.review** .

3. Insert a table with two columns and seven rows.

4. Type **Jobs** at the top of the first column.

5. Type **Computer Words** at the top of the second column.

6. Type the words from page 41 in the two columns.

Example:

Jobs	Computer Words

Highlighting and Using Bold

7. Make **Jobs** bold:

   • Highlight **Jobs**.

   • Click **B** .

8. Make **Computer Words** bold:

   • Highlight **Computer Words**.

   • Click **B** .

9. Save .

10. Close Microsoft Word **X** .

4.5 Typing: Italics

1. Open Microsoft Word .

2. Open **yourname.4.4.review** .

3. Italicize **Jobs**:

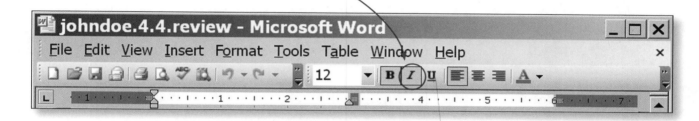

- Highlight **Jobs**.

- Click .

- Click on white space.

Jobs	Computer Words
mechanic	screen
doctor	mouse
homemaker	icon
dishwasher	keyboard
carpenter	pointer
cashier	disk

5. Save .

6. Close Microsoft Word .

4.6 Typing: Underline

1. Open Microsoft Word ![W] .

2. Open **yourname.4.4.review** ![icon] .

3. Underline **Computer Words**:

  • Highlight **Computer Words**.

  • Click ![U] .

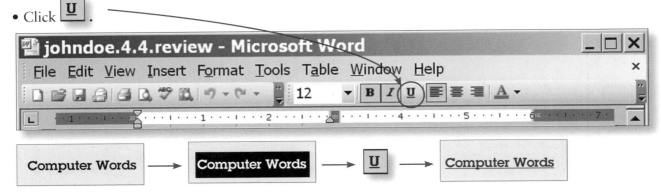

4. Click on white space.

5. Save ![icon] .

6. Close Microsoft Word ![X] .

4.7 Opening a New Microsoft Word Document

1. Open Microsoft Word ![W] .

2. Open **yourname.4.4.review** ![icon] .

3. Click ![icon] . Look at the new page.

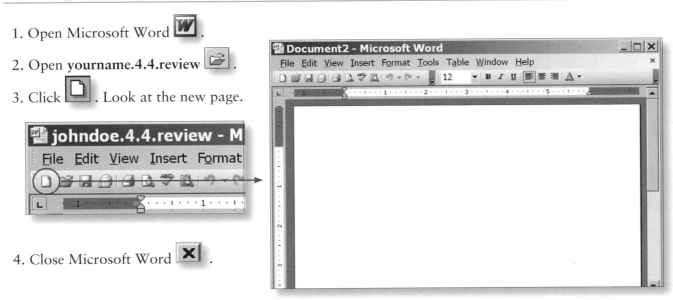

4. Close Microsoft Word ![X] .

Note to the Teacher: If students type in this new document, they will be prompted to save. See the online teacher's guide at www.outandaboutenglish.com for more information.

4.8 A Job List

Before You Start

Ask three classmates about their jobs:

What is your name?
What did you do in your country?
What do you do now?
What do you want to do in the future?

Write their answers:

Name	Past Job	Present Job	Future Job
Luke	teacher	mailman	computer programmer

A Job List

1. Open Microsoft Word .

2. Save the document as **yourname.4.8.jobs** .

3. Make this table:

Name	Past Job	Present Job	Future Job

4. Type the information from the **Before You Start** activity in the table.

5. Underline **Past Job** .

6. Italicize **Present Job** .

7. Bold **Future Job** .

8. Save .

9. Close Microsoft Word .

4.9 Typing: My Classmates

1. Open Microsoft Word .

2. Open **yourname.4.8.jobs** .

3. Type a paragraph about two classmates from **4.8 A Job List**.

4. Underline their names **U** .

5. Italicize their jobs **I** .

6. Save .

7. Close Microsoft Word **X** .

Example:

> <u>Luke</u> is a *student* now. He was a *teacher* in Korea. Now he is a *mailman*. He wants to be a *computer programmer* in the future.

4.10 My Portfolio: My Contact Information

1. Open Microsoft Word **W** .

2. Save the document as **yourname.4.10.mycontactinformation** .

3. Type the title: **About Me**.

4. Make **About Me** bold.

5. Type your name.

6. Type your address.

7. Type your telephone number.

8. Format the words. Use underline, bold, and italics.

9. Save .

10. Click **File**.

11. Click **Print Preview**.

12. Look. Is the document OK?

13. Click **Close**.

14. Click **File**.

15. Click **Print** .

16. Add this page to your portfolio.

17. Close Microsoft Word **X** .

Example:

> ***About Me***
>
> <u>**John Doe**</u>
> 21 Helwig Street
> Fort Worth, TX 20812
> *410.555.4432*

4.11 The Internet

Do you use the Internet? What can you find on the Internet? Write your answers. Tell your partner.

_____

_____

_____

4.12 Connecting to and Disconnecting from the Internet

Opening Internet Explorer (Connecting)

On your desktop, double-click

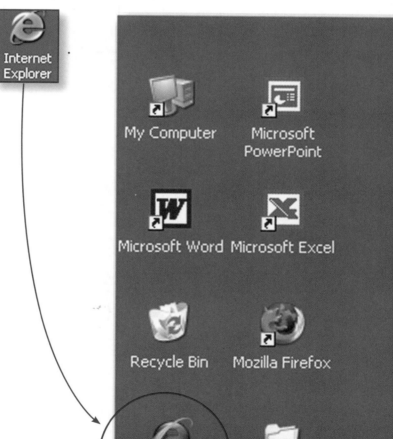

Closing Internet Explorer (Disconnecting)

Click **✕** .

Practice

1. Connect to the Internet .

2. Disconnect from the Internet **✕** .

3. Repeat steps 1 and 2.

4.13 The Internet: Opening a Web Site

1. Connect to the Internet .

2. Open the Web site:
   www.outandaboutenglish.com:

   • Click in the address field.

   • Press **Backspace** to erase.

   • Type www.outandaboutenglish.com.

   • Press **Enter**.

3. Disconnect from the Internet **✕** .

4.14 The Internet: Scrolling Up and Down in a Web Page

1. Connect to the Internet 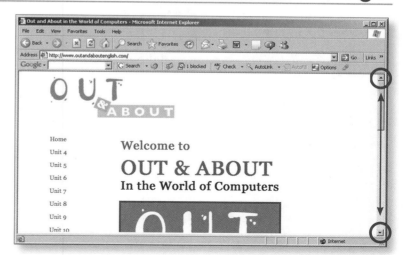.

2. Open the Web site: www.outandaboutenglish.com.

3. Click ▼ to scroll down.

4. Click ▲ to scroll up.

5. Disconnect from the Internet ✕.

4.15 The Internet: Jobs

1. Connect to the Internet .

2. Open the Web site: www.outandaboutenglish.com.

3. Click on **Unit 4.**

4. Scroll to the bottom.

5. Scroll to the top.

6. Look at the pictures. What do these people do?

7. Write the answers:

	Name	Job
a.	Bobbi	computer programmer
b.	Sally	
c.	Ted	
d.	Alice	
e.	Luke	
f.	Helen	

8. Disconnect from the Internet ✕.

4.16 The Internet: Work Schedules

1. Connect to the Internet 🅔 .

2. Open the Web site: www.outandaboutenglish.com.

3. Click **Unit 4.**

4. Scroll to the bottom.

5. Scroll to the top.

6. Read the work schedule.

7. Write the answers:

   a. When does the nurse work?   _____ Monday—Friday 9:00 a.m.—4:00 p.m. _____

   b. When does the mechanic work?   _____

   c. When does the server work?   _____

   d. When does the painter work?   _____

8. Disconnect from the Internet ❌ .

4.17 The Internet: Job Lists

1. Connect to the Internet 🅔 .

2. Open the Web site: **www.outandaboutenglish.com.**

3. Click **Unit 4.**

4. Scroll to the bottom.

5. Scroll to the top.

6. Read the job listings.

7. Write the answers below.

8. Disconnect from the Internet ❌ .

Date: _January 28_____

Job: _____

Hours: _____

City: _____

Date: _____

Job: _Journalist_____

Hours: _____

City: _____

Date: _____

Job: _____

Hours: _Monday—Friday: 9 a.m.—noon_

City: _____

Date: _____

Job: _____

Hours: _____

City: _Sarasota, FL_____

4.18 Homework

The Internet: A Web Page

1. Connect to the Internet.

2. Open the Web site: www.outandaboutenglish.com.

3. Click on **Unit 4.**

4. Scroll to the bottom.

5. Scroll to the top.

6. Look at the page. Write four words that you know:

_____ , _____ , _____ , _____

7. Find four new words. Write them here:

_____ , _____ , _____ , _____

8. What do the four words mean? (Ask a teacher. Ask a friend. Look in the dictionary.)

_____

_____

_____

_____

9. Disconnect from the Internet ☒ .

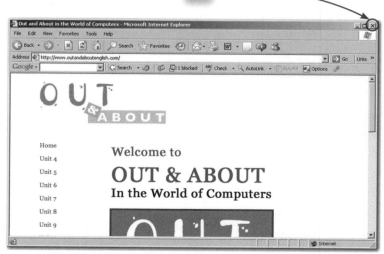

Unit 4 End-of-Unit Checklist

REVIEW		
I can . . .		
. . . open Microsoft Word documents.	☐ Yes!	☐ Not yet.
. . . save Microsoft Word documents.	☐ Yes!	☐ Not yet.
. . . insert tables.	☐ Yes!	☐ Not yet.
. . . highlight words.	☐ Yes!	☐ Not yet.
. . . use bold.	☐ Yes!	☐ Not yet.
. . . use print preview.	☐ Yes!	☐ Not yet.
UNIT 4		
I can . . .		
. . . italicize words.	☐ Yes!	☐ Not yet.
. . . underline words.	☐ Yes!	☐ Not yet.
. . . open new Microsoft Word documents.	☐ Yes!	☐ Not yet.
. . . connect to the Internet.	☐ Yes!	☐ Not yet.
. . . disconnect from the Internet.	☐ Yes!	☐ Not yet.
. . . open Web sites.	☐ Yes!	☐ Not yet.
. . . scroll up and down in Web pages.	☐ Yes!	☐ Not yet.

UNIT 5

This Is My Family.

5.1 Vocabulary

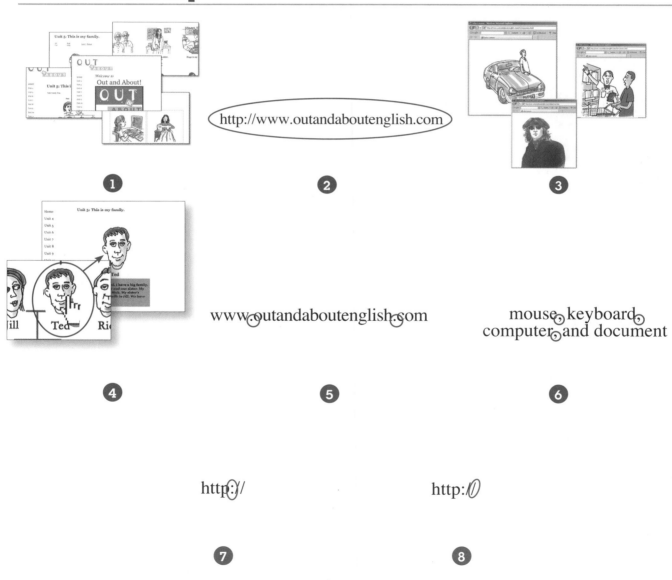

http://www.outandaboutenglish.com

1

2

3

www.outandaboutenglish.com

mouse, keyboard, computer, and document

4

5

6

http://

http:/

7

8

5.2 Speaking

PARTNER **A:** *Look at page 53.*

PARTNER **B:** *Look at page 54. Say the words.*

PARTNER **A:** *Point to the picture.*

Change roles and repeat.

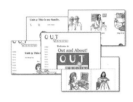

http://www.outandaboutenglish.com

1. Web site   **2. Web address**   **3. images (pictures)**

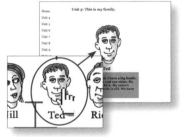

www.outandaboutenglish.com   mouse, keyboard, computer, and document

4. link   **5. dot (period)**   **6. comma**

http://   http://

7. colon   **8. slash**

5.3 Writing

Listen to your teacher. Write the words. Show your partner.

1. _____   5. _____

2. _____   6. _____

3. _____   7. _____

4. _____   8. _____

> **!** **IMPORTANT . . .**
>
> Sitting ⟶
>
>
>
> Sit straight.
> Put your feet flat on the floor.

5.4 Review

Before You Start

Write each word in the correct column below:

store	son	computer	hospital
screen	printer	daughter	farm
post office	brother	husband	monitor

Places	Computer Words	Family Words

Inserting a Table

1. Open Microsoft Word **W** .

2. Save the document as **yourname.5.4.review** 💾 .

3. Insert a table with three columns and five rows.

4. Type the words **Places, Computer Words,** and **Family Words** in the first row.

5. Type the words from the **Before You Start** activity in the three columns.

6. Save 💾 .

7. Close Microsoft Word **✕** .

Typing: Bold, Italics, Underline

1. Open Microsoft Word 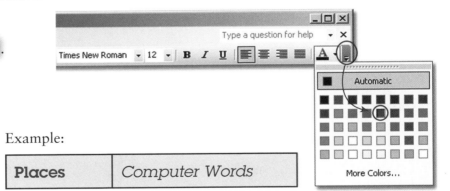.

2. Open **yourname.5.4.review**.

3. Make **Places** bold:

  • Highlight **Places**.

  • Click **B**.

4. Italicize **Computer Words**:

  • Highlight **Computer Words**.

  • Click **I**.

5. Underline **Family Words**:

  • Highlight **Family Words**.

  • Click **U**.

6. Save.

7. Close Microsoft Word.

Example:

Places	*Computer Words*	Family Words
store	screen	son
post office	printer	brother
hospital	computer	daughter
farm	monitor	

5.5 Typing: Changing Colors

1. Open Microsoft Word.

2. Open **yourname.5.4.review**.

3. Make **Places** blue:

  • Highlight **Places**.

  • Click **A**.

  • Click the blue square.

  • Click on white space.

Example:

Places	*Computer Words*

Practice

1. Make **Places** red.

2. Make **Computer Words** green.

3. Make **Family Words** orange.

4. Save.

5. Close Microsoft Word.

5.6 Typing: Making Words Bigger and Smaller

1. Open Microsoft Word 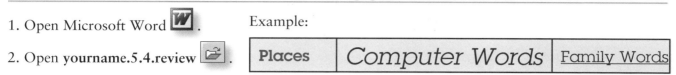.

2. Open **yourname.5.4.review** .

3. Make **Computer Words** size 18:

   • Highlight **Computer Words**.

   • Click .

   • Click 18.

   • Click on white space.

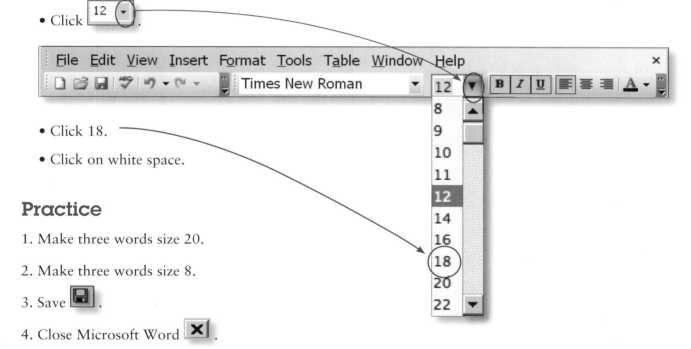

Practice

1. Make three words size 20.

2. Make three words size 8.

3. Save .

4. Close Microsoft Word .

5.7 My Portfolio: My Family

Before You Start

Listen to your teacher. Write the words. Show your partner.

Family

1. _____   6. _____

2. _____   7. _____

3. _____   8. _____

4. _____   9. _____

5. _____   10. _____

My Family

1. Open Microsoft Word  .

2. Save your document as
   yourname.5.7.myfamily 💾 .

3. Type 2–5 sentences about your family.

4. Change the size and color of some words.

   Example:

   > My sister is **tall** and **beautiful**. Her name is Angela.
   >
   > She has hazel eyes and brown hair.

5. Save 💾 .

6. Print 🖨 .

7. Add this page to your portfolio.

8. Close Microsoft Word ❌ .

5.8 My Portfolio: My Partner's Family

Before You Start

Interview your partner. Ask these questions:

> *Do you have a _____?*   *(sister/brother/son/daughter)*
>
> *What is _____ name?*   *(his/her)*
>
> *What does _____ look like?*   *(he/she)*

Example: Do you have a brother? What is his name? What does he look like?

Write about your partner's family:

Relationship	Name	Description

My Partner's Family

1. Open Microsoft Word .

2. Save the document as **yourname.5.8.partnersfamily** .

3. Make a table with three columns and four rows.

4. Type **Relationship, Name,** and **Description** in the first row.

5. Type the information from your interview in the table.

6. Change the size and color of the words.

Example:

Relationship	Name	Description
brother	Jacob	tall, thin, blue eyes, brown hair, moustache

7. Save .

8. Print .

9. Add this page to your portfolio.

10. Close Microsoft Word .

5.9 The Internet: Web Addresses

Listen to your teacher. Write the Web addresses:

> **Web Addresses**
>
> 1. _____
> 2. _____
> 3. _____
> 4. _____
> 5. _____

Answer the questions:

1. Are there any spaces in the Web addresses?   Yes   No

2. Are there dots, colons, slashes, and underscores in Web addresses? Yes   No

3. What do Web addresses start with? _____

4. What do Web addresses end with? _____

Repeat the Web addresses to your partner. Write them again:

> **Web Addresses**
>
> 1. _____
> 2. _____
> 3. _____
> 4. _____
> 5. _____

What's wrong? Circle the problems. Write the correct address:

Wrong Web Address	Correct Web Address
http:Wwwhotmailcom	
http//www yahoo com	
http://outandaboutenglish	
www,google,com	

5.10 The Internet: Review

Connecting to and Disconnecting from the Internet

1. Open Internet Explorer:

   • Double-click 🌐 .

2. Close Internet Explorer:

   • Click ❌ .

Opening a Web Site

1. Connect to the Internet 🌐 .

2. Click in the address field.

3. Type www.outandaboutenglish.com.

4. Press **Enter**.

5. Disconnect from the Internet ❌ .

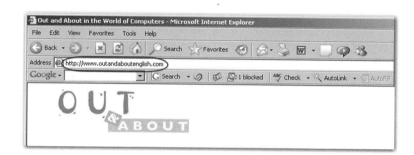

Scrolling Up and Down in a Web Page

1. Connect to the Internet 🌐 .

2. Open the Web site:
   www.outandaboutenglish.com.

3. Click 🔽 to scroll down.

4. Click 🔼 to scroll up.

5. Disconnect from the Internet ❌ .

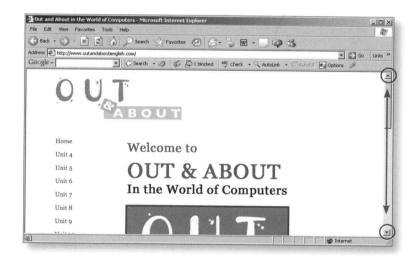

5.11 The Internet: Images

Before You Start

Listen to your teacher. Write three Web addresses:

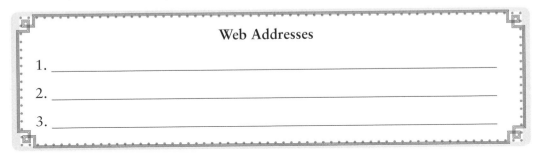

Web Addresses

1. _____

2. _____

3. _____

Images

1. Connect to the Internet 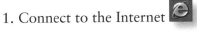 .

2. Go to the three Web sites.

3. How many images do you see?
   Write the information in the table:

Web Address	Number of Images

4. Disconnect from the Internet ❌ .

5.12 The Internet: An Image Link

1. Connect to the Internet .

2. Open the Web site:
   www.outandaboutenglish.com.

3. Click **Unit 5.** Scroll Down.

4. Click on **Ted** .

5. Read about Ted.

6. Disconnect from the Internet ❌ .

Ted's Family Tree:

Rose   Bob

Jill   Ted   Rick   Amy

Brian   Dana

5.13 The Internet: Using the Back Button

1. Connect to the Internet .

2. Open the Web site:
   www.outandaboutenglish.com.

3. Click **Unit 5.**

4. Click **Ted** .

5. Click Back .

6. Click Amy . Read about Amy.

7. Click Back .

8. Click Rick . Read about Rick.

9. Click Back .

10. Click Jill . Read about Jill.

11. Click Back .

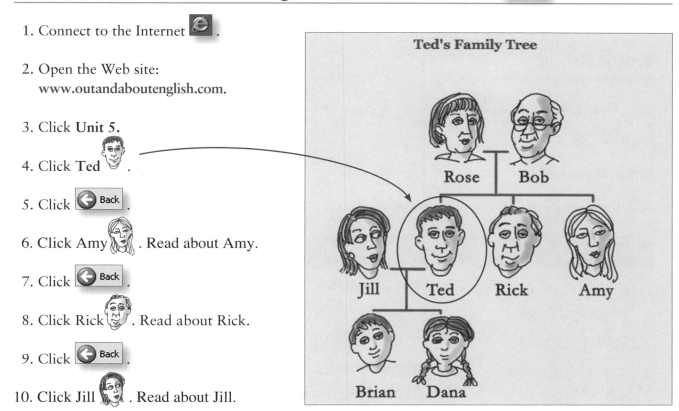

Ted's Family Tree

Rose   Bob

Jill   Ted   Rick   Amy

Brian   Dana

http://www.outandaboutenglish.com

File Edit View Favorites Tools Help

Back ▼   Search ☆ Favorites

Address http://www.outandaboutenglish.com

12. What page do you see?

    Write the Web address here: _____

13. Disconnect from the Internet .

5.14 The Internet: Following Image Links

1. Connect to the Internet 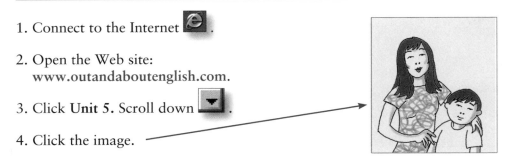.

2. Open the Web site:
   www.outandaboutenglish.com.

3. Click **Unit 5.** Scroll down .

4. Click the image.

5. Follow the image links.

6. Who are these people? Write the answers:

Name	Relationship	Age
	Carol's husband	
Hugo and Robert		
Esther		
	Carol's father	
	Carol's grandmother	
Lizzy		

7. Disconnect from the Internet .

5.15 The Internet: Searching for Images

1. Connect to the Internet .

2. Open the Web site:
   www.google.com.

3. Click Images .

4. Type **John Lennon.**

5. Click Search Images .

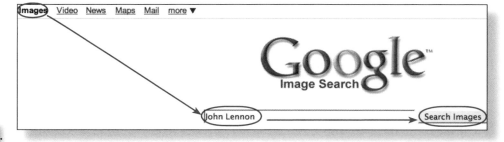

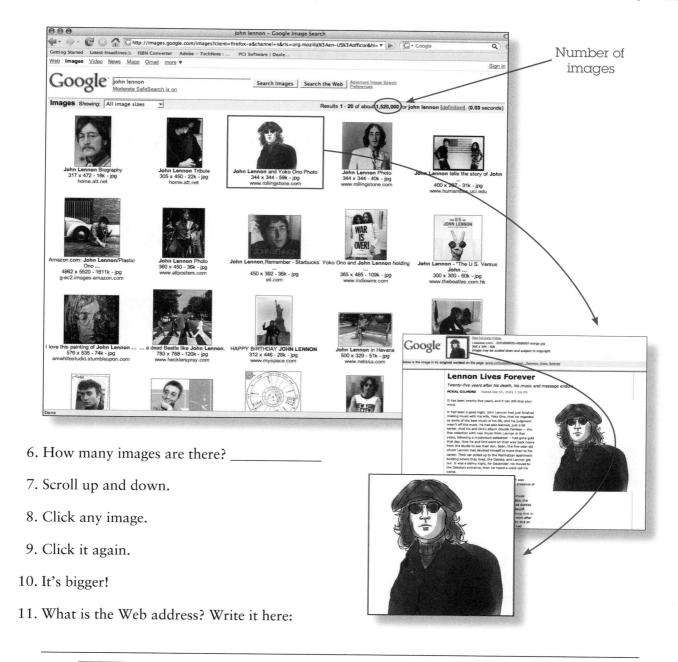

Number of images

6. How many images are there? _____

7. Scroll up and down.

8. Click any image.

9. Click it again.

10. It's bigger!

11. What is the Web address? Write it here:

_____

12. Click [⬅ Back] two times.

13. Repeat steps 8–10.

14. What is the Web address? Write it here:

_____

15. Click [⬅ Back] two times.

16. Disconnect from the Internet [✖].

5.16 The Internet: Famous People

Before You Start

Ask your partner:

> *Who is your favorite actor or actress? (How do you spell that?)*
>
> *Who is your favorite musician?*

Write the answers:

> *Favorite actor or actress:* _____
>
> *Favorite musician:* _____

Famous People

Favorite Actress or Actor

1. Connect to the Internet .

2. Open the Web site: **www.google.com**.

3. Click **Images** .

4. Type the name of your partner's favorite actor or actress.

5. Click **Search Images** .

6. Write the number of images in the table below.

7. Show your partner.

8. Click one image two times.

9. Write the Web address in the table below.

Favorite Musician

1. Open the Web site: **www.google.com**.

2. Click **Images** .

3. Type the name of your partner's favorite musician.

4. Click **Search Images** .

5. Write the number of images in the table below.

6. Show your partner.

7. Click one image two times.

8. Write the Web address in the table below.

9. Disconnect from the Internet **✕** .

Actress or Actor	Number of Images	Web Address
Musician	**Number of Images**	**Web Address**

5.17 My Portfolio: Who is Famous in Your Native Country?

Before You Start

Ask three classmates:

> *What's your name?*
>
> *Who is famous in your native country? (How do you spell that?)*

Write the answers:

Name	Famous Person

Who is Famous in Your Native Country?

1. Open Microsoft Word .
2. Save the document as **yourname.5.17.famouspeople** .
3. Make this table.
4. Type the names of famous people.
5. Search for images of famous people.
6. Type the number of images.

7. Type the Web addresses.
8. Change the color and size of the words. Use underline, bold, and italics.
9. Save .
10. Print .
11. Add this page to your portfolio.
12. Close Microsoft Word .

Famous Person	Number of Images	Web Address

5.18 Homework

The Internet: Image Links

1. Ask your friends, family, or teacher for a Web address.
2. Write the Web address:

   _____

3. Connect to the Internet .
4. Click in the address text box.

5. Type the Web address.
6. Press **Enter**.
7. How many images are on the Web page? _____
8. How many images are links? _____
9. Disconnect from the Internet .

Unit 5 End-of-Unit Checklist

REVIEW		
I can . . .		
. . . insert tables.	☐ Yes!	☐ Not yet.
. . . use bold.	☐ Yes!	☐ Not yet.
. . . italicize words.	☐ Yes!	☐ Not yet.
. . . underline words.	☐ Yes!	☐ Not yet.
. . . connect to the Internet.	☐ Yes!	☐ Not yet.
. . . disconnect from the Internet.	☐ Yes!	☐ Not yet.
. . . open Web sites.	☐ Yes!	☐ Not yet.
. . . scroll up and down in Web pages.	☐ Yes!	☐ Not yet.
UNIT 5		
I can . . .		
. . . change the color of words.	☐ Yes!	☐ Not yet.
. . . make words bigger and smaller.	☐ Yes!	☐ Not yet.
. . . write Web addresses.	☐ Yes!	☐ Not yet.
. . . use the Back button.	☐ Yes!	☐ Not yet.
. . . search for images on the Internet.	☐ Yes!	☐ Not yet.
. . . use www.google.com to find information.	☐ Yes!	☐ Not yet.

UNIT 6

This Is My House.

6.1 Vocabulary

http://

1

http://

2

t-shirt

3

english_unit1

4

5

6

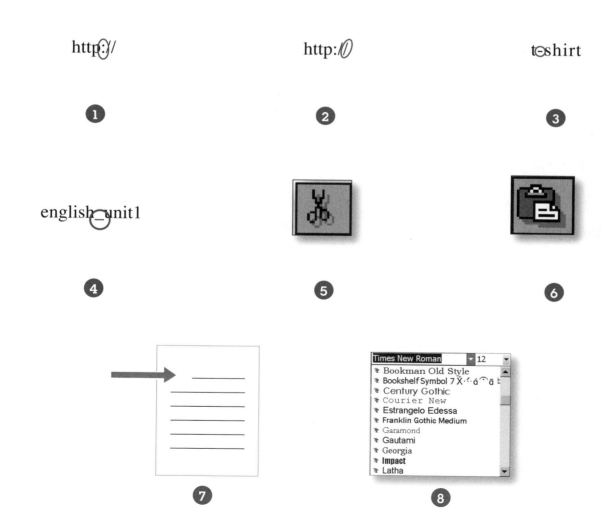

7

Times New Roman   12
- Bookman Old Style
- Bookshelf Symbol 7 X·⸱·á⌒ā b
- Century Gothic
- Courier New
- Estrangelo Edessa
- Franklin Gothic Medium
- Garamond
- Gautami
- Georgia
- Impact
- Latha

8

6.2 Speaking

PARTNER **A:** *Look at page 69.*

PARTNER **B:** *Look at page 70. Say the words.*

PARTNER **A:** *Point to the picture.*

Change roles and repeat.

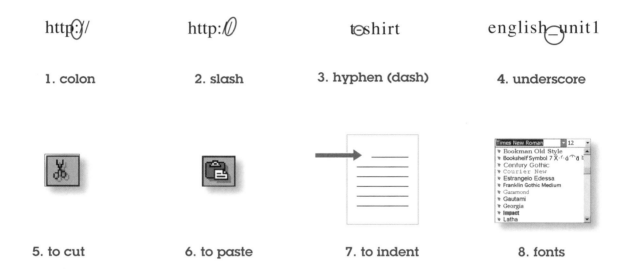

http://	http://	t-shirt	english_unit1
1. colon	2. slash	3. hyphen (dash)	4. underscore
5. to cut	6. to paste	7. to indent	8. fonts

6.3 Writing

Listen to your teacher. Write the words. Show your partner.

1. _____   5. _____

2. _____   6. _____

3. _____   7. _____

4. _____   8. _____

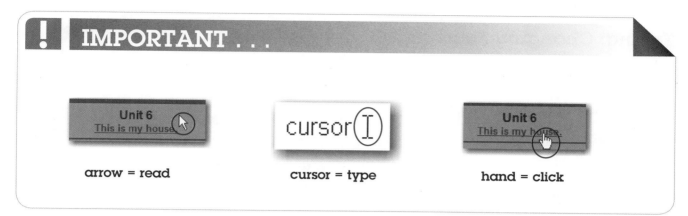

! IMPORTANT . . .

arrow = read　　　cursor = type　　　hand = click

6.4 Review

Making Words Bigger and Smaller

1. Open Microsoft Word [W].

2. Save the document as **yourname.6.4.review** [💾].

3. Type **Isabel is thin. She has green eyes. She has blond hair. She is 60 years old.**

4. Make the words bigger and smaller. Use bold, italics, and underline.

File Edit View Insert Format Tools Table Window Help

Example:

Isabel **is** thin. She has *green* eyes. She <u>has</u> *blond* hair. She **is** 60 **years old**.

5. Save [💾].

6. Close Microsoft Word [✕].

6.5 Typing: Changing Fonts

Before You Start

Write 3–5 sentences about two friends.

Example:

Isabel is thin. She has green eyes. She has blond hair. She is 60 years old.

Max is tall and heavy. He has short, dark, curly hair. He has a beard.

_____

_____

_____

Typing: Changing Fonts

1. Open **Microsoft Word** 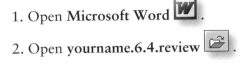.

2. Open **yourname.6.4.review** .

3. Make **Isabel** Comic Sans MS:

   - Highlight **Isabel**.

   - Click Times New Roman .

   - Click **Comic Sans MS.**

   - Click on white space.

4. Type the descriptions of your two friends.

5. Change the fonts of five more words.

6. Save .

7. Close Microsoft Word .

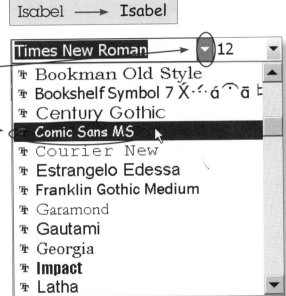

Isabel ⟶ Isabel

6.6 Cutting and Pasting

Cutting

1. Open Microsoft Word .

2. Save the document as **yourname.6.6.furniture** .

3. Type these words: chair lamp sofa sink mirror

4. Cut **Chair**:

   - Highlight **Chair**.

   - Click **Edit**.

   - Click **Cut**.

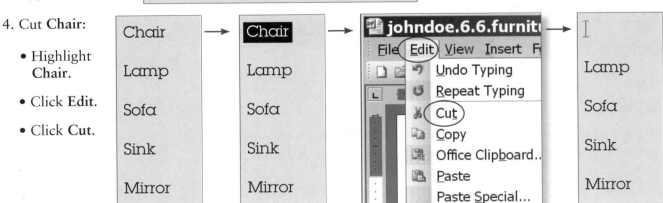

Pasting

5. Paste **Chair:**

- Move the cursor.
- Click **Edit.**
- Click **Paste.**

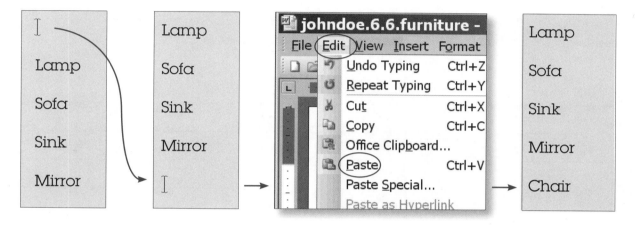

6. Look at your new list.

7. Save  .

8. Close Microsoft Word  .

6.7 Inserting a Table: My Furniture

1. Open Microsoft Word 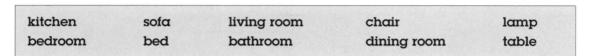.

2. Save the document as **yourname.6.7.furnituretable** .

3. Type these words:

kitchen	sofa	living room	chair	lamp
bedroom	bed	bathroom	dining room	table

4. Insert this table:

Rooms	Furniture

5. Cut **kitchen** and paste it into the **Rooms** column.

Example:

kitchen	sofa	living room	chair	lamp
bedroom	bed	bathroom	dining room	table

Rooms	Furniture
kitchen	

6. Cut and paste the other words into the correct columns.

7. Check your work with a partner.

8. Save .

9. Close Microsoft Word .

6.8 Indenting

1. Open Microsoft Word 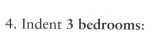.

2. Save the document as **yourname.6.8.annshouse** 🖫.

3. Type these words:

> Ann's house
> 3 bedrooms
> 2 bathrooms
> 1 living room
> no dining room
> yard

4. Indent **3 bedrooms**:

   • Put the cursor before the **3**.

   • Press **Tab**.

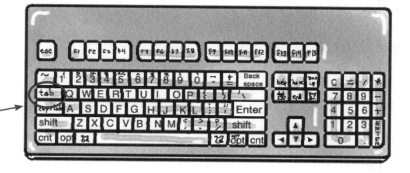

Practice

1. Indent **2 bathrooms**.

2. Indent **1 living room**.

3. Indent **no dining room**.

4. Indent **yard.**

5. Save 🖫.

6. Close ❌.

> Ann's house
> 3 bedrooms
> 2 bathrooms
> 1 living room
> no dining room
> yard

→

> Ann's house
>   3 bedrooms
>   2 bathrooms
>   1 living room
>   no dining room
>   yard

6.9 Typing: My Partner's House

Before You Start

Interview your partner. Ask these questions:

> *How many bedrooms do you have?* _____
>
> *How many bathrooms do you have?* _____
>
> *Do you have a living room?* _____
>
> *Do you have a dining room?* _____
>
> *Do you have a yard?* _____

My Partner's House

1. Open Microsoft Word .

2. Save the document as **yourname.6.9.partnershouse** .

3. Type and indent the answers.

4. Save .

5. Close Microsoft Word .

Example:

> **Mike's House**
>
> 2 bedrooms
>
> 1 bathroom
>
> 1 living room
>
> 1 dining room
>
> no yard

6.10 Typing: A Paragraph

1. Open Microsoft Word .

2. Open **yourname.6.9.partnershouse** .

3. Type a paragraph about your partner's house. Use the information in your document.

4. Indent the first word:
   - Put the cursor before the first word.
   - Press **Tab.**

5. Save .

6. Close Microsoft Word .

Example:

> Mike lives in an apartment. His apartment has two bedrooms. It has a living room, a bathroom, and a dining room. There is no yard.

6.11 My Portfolio: Activities in My Home

Before You Start

What do you do in these rooms? Write your answers:

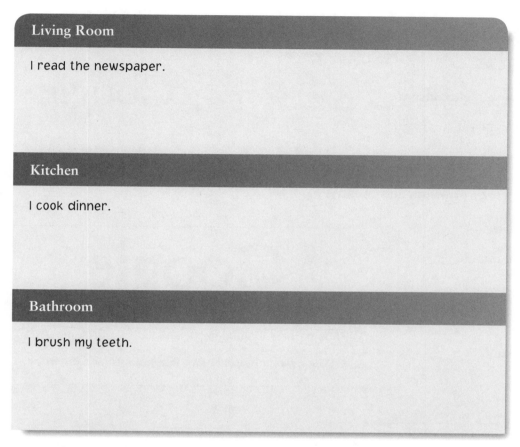

Living Room

I read the newspaper.

Kitchen

I cook dinner.

Bathroom

I brush my teeth.

Activities in My Home

1. Open Microsoft Word 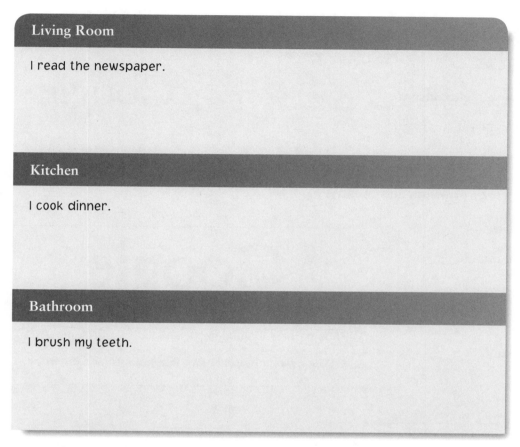.

2. Save the document as **yourname.6.11.myhomeactivities.**

3. Type three paragraphs about what you do in your home.

4. Save .

5. Print .

6. Add this page to your portfolio.

7. Close Microsoft Word .

Example:

> I read the newspaper in the living room. After dinner I watch TV. Sometimes I sleep on the sofa.
>
> I cook and wash dishes in the kitchen. I eat breakfast and dinner there. I sit at the table and talk to my family.
>
> I brush my teeth in the bathroom. I take a shower every day. I take a bath on Sunday. I wash my hands before breakfast and dinner. I use the toilet too.

6.12 The Internet: Review

Before You Start

Where were you born? _____

Searching for Images

1. Connect to the Internet  .

2. Open the Web site www.google.com.

3. Find an image of your hometown:

   • Click **Images** .

   • Type the city name, state or province, and country.

   • Click **Search Images** .

   • How many images are there? _____

   • Look for an image that you like.

   • Click on the image.

   • Click on the image again.

   • Write the Web address:

4. Show your partner.

5. Click **Back** two times.

6. Look for two more cities.
   Write the information in the table:

City	Number of Images	Web Address of One Image

7. Ask your partner: What cities did you see? How many images?

Note to the Teacher: If students can't find an image of their city, see the online teacher's guide at www.outandaboutenglish.com for suggestions.

6.13 The Internet: Following Word Links

1. Connect to the Internet  .

2. Open the Web site: **www.outandaboutenglish.com.**

3. Click **Unit 6.**

4. Find word links.

5. Circle the words that are links:

News	The Out and About Times	Classifieds	Sports	Weather

6. Click on **Classifieds.**

7. Find the following information. Write the answers:

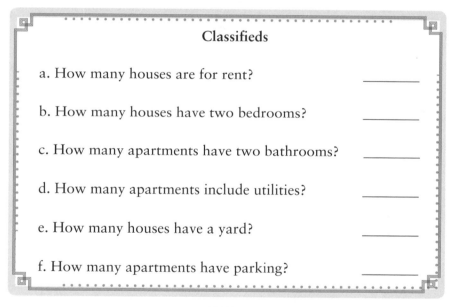

Classifieds

a. How many houses are for rent? _____

b. How many houses have two bedrooms? _____

c. How many apartments have two bathrooms? _____

d. How many apartments include utilities? _____

e. How many houses have a yard? _____

f. How many apartments have parking? _____

8. Disconnect from the Internet ☒ .

6.14 The Internet: Classifieds

1. Connect to the Internet 🅮 .

2. Open the Web site: www.outandaboutenglish.com.

3. Click on **Unit 6**.

4. Read the following:

> Bob and Jim live in an apartment in the city. They want
> a new sofa for the living room. Find a sofa for sale in the
> classifieds. Write about the sofa:

Sofa	
Color:	_____
Size:	_____
Price:	_____
Telephone Number:	_____

> Carol is a gardener. She needs to buy a new truck for her
> job. Find a truck in the classifieds. Write about the truck:

Truck	
Make:	_____
Year:	_____
Model:	_____
Price:	_____
Telephone Number:	_____

5. Disconnect from the Internet ❌ .

6.15 Homework

The Internet: Word Links

1. Look at the food packages in your kitchen to find a Web address.

2. Write the Web address:

   _____

3. Connect to the Internet  .

4. Click in the address text box.

5. Type the Web address.

6. Press **Enter**.

7. How many word links are on the Web page? _____

8. Disconnect from the Internet **⊠** .

Before You Start

Listen to your teacher. Write the name of the local newspaper: _____

Write the Web address of the local newspaper: _____

The Internet: Rental Ads

1. Connect to the Internet **e** .

2. Open the Web site.

3. Follow the word links to the rental ads.

4. Find one apartment or house that you like.

5. Answer the questions.

6. Write five words you don't know:

> **Rental Ads**
>
> How many bedrooms are there? _____
>
> How many bathrooms are there? _____
>
> Does it include utilities? _____
>
> Is there a yard? _____

_____ _____ _____

_____ _____

7. Disconnect from the Internet **⊠** .

8. Open Microsoft Word **W** .

9. Save the document as **yourname.6.15.rentalads** 💾 .

10. Type a paragraph about the house or apartment.

11. Save 💾 .

12. Close Microsoft Word **⊠** .

Unit 6 End-of-Unit Checklist

REVIEW

I can . . .

. . . make words bigger and smaller.	☐ Yes!	☐ Not yet.
. . . insert tables.	☐ Yes!	☐ Not yet.
. . . use www.google.com to find information.	☐ Yes!	☐ Not yet.
. . . search for images on the Internet.	☐ Yes!	☐ Not yet.
. . . follow image links.	☐ Yes!	☐ Not yet.
. . . use the Back button.	☐ Yes!	☐ Not yet.

UNIT 6

I can . . .

. . . change fonts.	☐ Yes!	☐ Not yet.
. . . cut.	☐ Yes!	☐ Not yet.
. . . paste.	☐ Yes!	☐ Not yet.
. . . indent.	☐ Yes!	☐ Not yet.
. . . type paragraphs.	☐ Yes!	☐ Not yet.
. . . follow word links.	☐ Yes!	☐ Not yet.

UNIT 7

What Do You Want to Eat?

7.1 Vocabulary

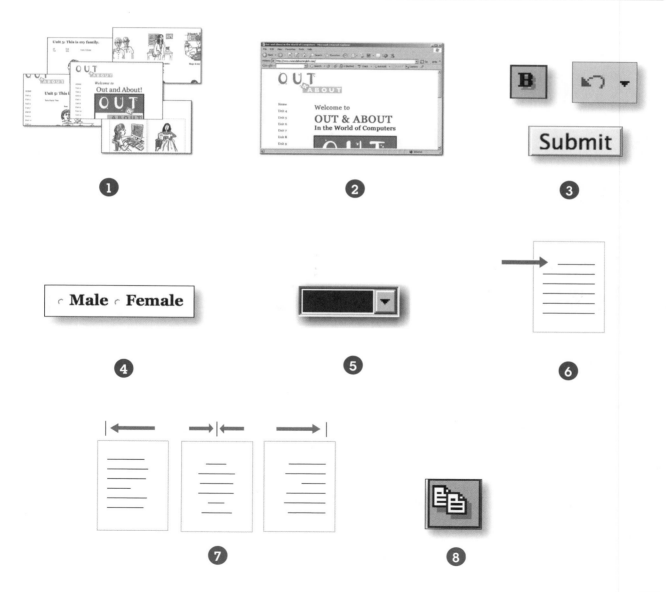

7.2 Speaking

PARTNER A: *Look at page 83.*

PARTNER B: *Look at page 84. Say the words.*

PARTNER A: *Point to the picture.*

Change roles and repeat.

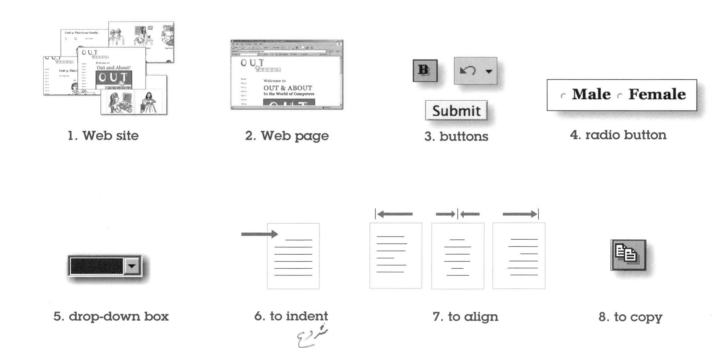

1. Web site

2. Web page

3. buttons

4. radio button

5. drop-down box

6. to indent

7. to align

8. to copy

7.3 Writing

Listen to your teacher. Write the words. Show your partner.

1. _____   5. _____

2. _____   6. _____

3. _____   7. _____

4. _____   8. _____

! IMPORTANT . . .

Rest your eyes and hands every five minutes!

Look away.

Shake your hands.

7.4 Review

Before You Start

Write each word in the correct column below:

| juice | water | potatoes | onions | cookies |
| tomatoes | soup | beans | rice | soda |

Can	Bottle	Bag

Cutting and Pasting

1. Open Microsoft Word .

2. Save the document as **yourname.7.4.review**  .

3. Type these words:

| juice | water | potatoes | onions | cookies |
| tomatoes | soup | beans | rice | soda |

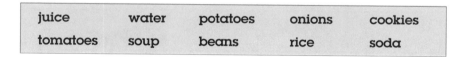

4. Create a table with two columns and three rows.

5. Type the questions in the table.

Example:

What can you buy in a can?	
What can you buy in a bottle?	
What can you buy in a bag?	

6. Cut and paste the food and drink words into the correct cells:

Cutting

- Highlight.
- Click **Edit**.
- Click **Cut**.

Pasting

- Move the cursor.
- Click **Edit**.
- Click **Paste**.

7. Save 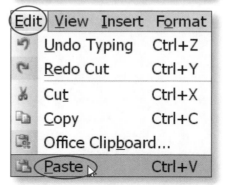 .

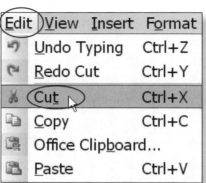

Example:

What can you buy in a can?	soup, tomatoes, beans
What can you buy in a bottle?	soda, water, juice
What can you buy in a bag?	potatoes, onions, rice, cookies

Note to the Teacher: Some food and drink words may belong in more than one category. See the online teacher's guide at www.outandaboutenglish.com for more information.

Formatting

8. Format the words in the document **yourname.7.4.review**. Change:

- font
- size
- bold
- italics
- underline
- color

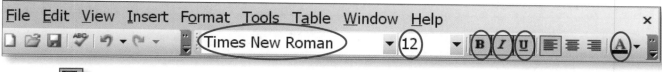

9. Save .

10. Close Microsoft Word .

7.5 Copying and Pasting

1. Open Microsoft Word .

2. Open **yourname.7.4.review** .

3. Copy **beans**:

- Highlight **beans**.
- Click **Edit**.
- Click **Copy**.

4. Paste **beans**:

- Move the cursor.
- Click **Edit**.
- Click **Paste**.

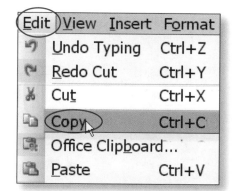

Example:

What can you buy in a can?	soup, tomatoes, **beans**
What can you buy in a bottle?	*soda, water, juice*
What can you buy in a bag?	potatoes, **onions**, rice, cookies, beans

5. Copy and paste **juice**:

What can you buy in a can?	soup, tomatoes, beans, juice beans
What can you buy in a bottle?	*soda, water,* juice
What can you buy in a bag?	potatoes, **onions**, rice, cookies, beans

6. Copy and paste **tomatoes**:

What can you buy in a can?	soup, tomatoes beans, juice beans
What can you buy in a bottle?	*soda, water, juice,* tomatoes
What can you buy in a bag?	potatoes, **onions**, rice, cookies, beans

7. Save  .

8. Close Microsoft Word  .

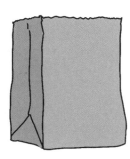

7.6 Typing: At the Supermarket

Before You Start

Ask your partner:

What can you buy in a _____ ?

What can you buy by the _____ ?

Write the answers:

bag	box	bottle	bunch	can
pound	**loaf**	**head**	**dozen**	**gallon**

What can you buy at the supermarket? Write a paragraph. Use some of these words:

box	bag	bottle	bunch	pound
loaf	head	dozen	gallon	can

Example:

I can buy bananas in a bunch. I can buy . . .

_____

_____

_____

_____

At the Supermarket

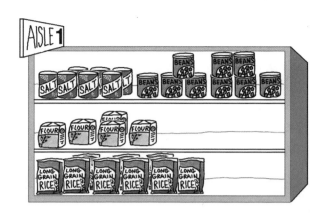

1. Open Microsoft Word .

2. Save the document as **yourname.7.6.foodcontainers** .

3. Type your paragraph.

4. Indent the first word.

5. Type your name at the top.

6. Type the date.

7. Type your teacher's name.

8. Type the title: **At the Supermarket.**

9. Make **At the Supermarket** bold.

10. Change the colors of the food words.

11. Make the food words italic.

12. Save .

13. Close Microsoft Word .

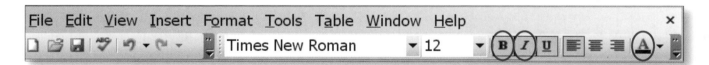

Example:

John Doe

February 11, 2025

Instructor: Tina Sander

At the Supermarket

    I can buy *bananas* in a bunch. I can buy *soup* in a can. I can buy *crackers* and *cereal* in a box. I can buy a dozen *eggs* and a dozen *cookies*. I can buy *juice* and *milk* by the gallon. I can buy *fruit* and *vegetables* by the pound.

7.7 Centering Words

1. Open Microsoft Word .

2. Open **yourname.7.6.foodcontainers** .

3. Center **At the Supermarket**:

- Highlight **At the Supermarket**.

- Click .

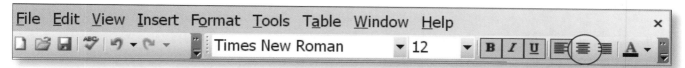

Example:

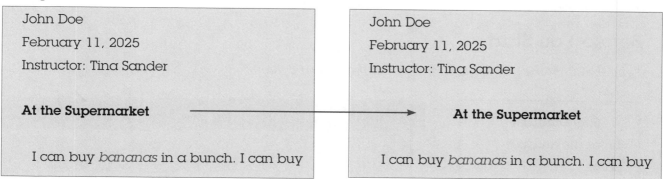

John Doe	John Doe
February 11, 2025	February 11, 2025
Instructor: Tina Sander	Instructor: Tina Sander
At the Supermarket	**At the Supermarket**
I can buy *bananas* in a bunch. I can buy	I can buy *bananas* in a bunch. I can buy

4. Save .

5. Close Microsoft Word .

7.8 Aligning Words to the Right

1. Open Microsoft Word .

2. Open **yourname.7.6.foodcontainers** .

3. Align your name, the date, and your teacher's name to the right:

- Highlight your name, the date, and your teacher's name.

- Click .

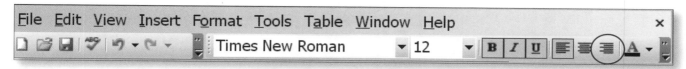

Example:

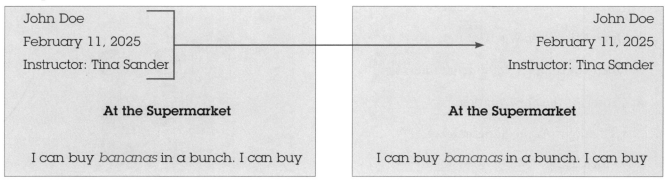

4. Save [save icon].

5. Close Microsoft Word [X icon] .

7.9 Aligning Words to the Left

Before You Start

Read the shopping list. Write each word in the correct column:

Shopping List
an apple/apples
corn
an onion/onions
an egg/eggs
milk
sugar
a potato/potatoes
a banana/bananas
salt
water

Count Noun	Noncount Nouns
an apple/apples	

Aligning Words to the Left

1. Open Microsoft Word 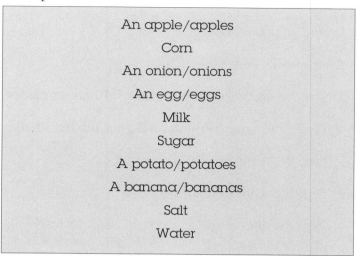.

2. Open **yourname.7.6.foodcontainers** .

3. Type the food words after your paragraph.

4. Center the words:

   • Highlight the words.

   • Click .

Example:

An apple/apples

Corn

An onion/onions

An egg/eggs

Milk

Sugar

A potato/potatoes

A banana/bananas

Salt

Water

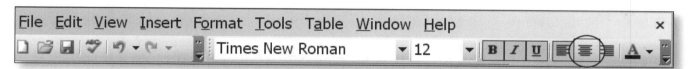

5. Align the count nouns to the left:

   • Highlight a count noun.

   • Click .

6. Align the noncount nouns to the right:

   • Highlight a noncount noun.

   • Click .

7. Save .

8. Close Microsoft Word .

Example:

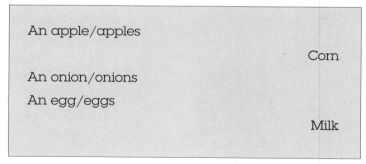

An apple/apples

Corn

An onion/onions

An egg/eggs

Milk

7.10 My Portfolio: A Favorite Recipe

1. Find your favorite recipe.

2. Open Microsoft Word 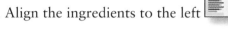.

3. Save the document as **yourname.7.10.favoriterecipe** .

4. Type your name, the date, and your teacher's name. Align them to the right .

5. Type the name of your recipe. Center it .

6. Type the word **Ingredients**.

7. Type the ingredients.

8. Align the ingredients to the left .

9. Indent the ingredients:
   - Put the cursor before an ingredient.
   - Press **Tab**.

10. Type the word **Instructions**.

11. Type the instructions.

12. Format the words.

13. Save .

14. Print .

15. Add this page to your portfolio.

16. Close Microsoft Word .

Example:

John Doe
January 20, 2035
Instructor: Tina Sander

Broccoli, Chickpea, and Tomato Salad

Ingredients

1 bag of tomatoes
1 can of chick peas
1 head of broccoli
1 tablespoon mustard
2 tablespoons red wine vinegar
2 tablespoons olive oil
1/2 red onion
salt and pepper

Instructions

1. Cut the broccoli and tomato.
2. Chop the red onion.
3. Steam the broccoli.
4. Mix mustard, vinegar, olive oil, red onion, salt and pepper.
5. Add tomatoes, chickpeas, and broccoli.
6. Stir.

7.11 The Internet: My Partner's Food

Before You Start

Ask your partner:

> *What country are you from?* _____
>
> *What food is popular?* _____

My Partner's Food

1. Connect to the Internet .

2. Open the web site: www.google.com.

3. Find images of the food from your partner's native country.

4. Show the images to your partner.

5. Write the information in the table:

Food	Number of Images	One Web Address

6. Disconnect from the Internet .

7.12 The Internet: Using Drop-down Boxes

1. Connect to the Internet .

2. Open the Web site:
   www.outandaboutenglish.com.

3. Click **Unit 7.**

4. Click **The Animal/The Meat.**

5. Read the questions.

6. Click the drop-down boxes.
   Answer the questions:

   • Click .

   • Click the answer.

7. Write your answers here.

1. What's *cow meat* in English?

[Select an Answer] ▾

[Select an Answer]
beef
pork
chicken
fish

My Answers

1. _____

2. _____

3. _____

8. Click [Check it out!].

9. Are your answers right? Show your partner. Correct your answers.

10. Disconnect from the Internet [✖] .

7.13 The Internet: What's your favorite . . .?

1. Connect to the Internet [e] .

2. Open the Web site: www.outandaboutenglish.com.

3. Click **Unit 7**.

4. Click **What's your favorite . . .?**

5. Read the questions.

6. Answer the questions:
   - Click [▼] .
   - Click the answer.

7. Click [Check it out!].

8. Write your answers here.

9. Show your partner.

10. Write your partner's answers here.

11. Disconnect from the Internet [✖] .

My Answers

Favorite Fruit: _____

Favorite Vegetable: _____

Favorite Drink: _____

My Partner's Answers

Favorite Fruit: _____

Favorite Vegetable: _____

Favorite Drink: _____

7.14 The Internet: Using Radio Buttons

1. Connect to the Internet 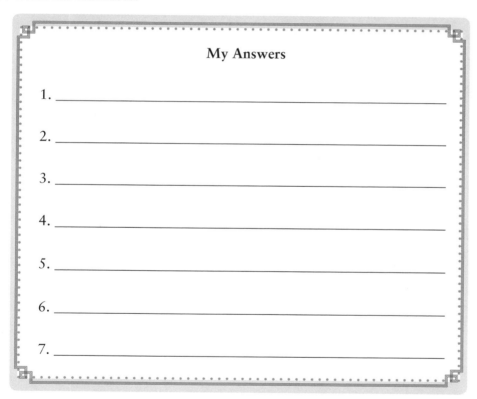.

2. Open the Web site: **www.outandaboutenglish.com**.

3. Click on **Unit 7**.

4. Click on **What do you have?**

5. Answer the questions:

   • Click `yes  no`.

6. Click `Check it out!`.

7. Write the sentences:

```
                              My Answers

      1. _____

      2. _____

      3. _____

      4. _____

      5. _____

      6. _____

      7. _____
```

8. Show your partner.

9. Disconnect from the Internet ☒.

Note to the Teacher: See the online teacher's guide at www.outandaboutenglish.com for writing extensions to this activity.

7.15 The Internet: Forms

1. Connect to the Internet  .

2. Open the Web site: www.outandaboutenglish.com.

3. Click **Unit 7**.

4. Click on **Personal Information**.

5. How many buttons are on the Web page? _____

6. How many drop-down boxes are on the Web page? _____

7. How many radio buttons are on the Web page? _____

8. Answer the questions on the Web page.

9. Click [Check it out!] .

10. Write the sentences:

> **My Answers**
>
> 1. _____
>
> 2. _____
>
> 3. _____
>
> 4. _____
>
> 5. _____
>
> 6. _____
>
> 7. _____
>
> 8. _____

11. Show your partner.

12. Disconnect from the Internet [×] .

7.16 Homework

Before You Start

Listen to your teacher. Write the name of a supermarket:

_____

Write the Web address of the supermarket:

_____

The Internet: A Supermarket

1. Connect to the Internet  .

2. Open the Web site.

3. Look at the Web page.

4. Write 10 food words:

Food Words

1. _____   6. _____

2. _____   7. _____

3. _____   8. _____

4. _____   9. _____

5. _____   10. _____

---

5. Disconnect from the Internet ☒ .

6. Open Microsoft Word 🄦 .

7. Save the document as **yourname.7.16.supermarketwords** 💾 .

8. Type the 10 food words.

9. Save 💾 .

10. Close Microsoft Word ☒ .

Unit 7 End-of-Unit Checklist

REVIEW		
I can . . .		
. . . cut and paste.	☐ Yes!	☐ Not yet.
. . . format words (change the font, size, and color).	☐ Yes!	☐ Not yet.
. . . type paragraphs.	☐ Yes!	☐ Not yet.
. . . indent.	☐ Yes!	☐ Not yet.
. . . search for images on the Internet.	☐ Yes!	☐ Not yet.
. . . use www.google.com to find information.	☐ Yes!	☐ Not yet.
. . . follow image and word links.	☐ Yes!	☐ Not yet.
UNIT 7		
I can . . .		
. . . copy and paste.	☐ Yes!	☐ Not yet.
. . . center words.	☐ Yes!	☐ Not yet.
. . . align words to the right.	☐ Yes!	☐ Not yet.
. . . align words to the left.	☐ Yes!	☐ Not yet.
. . . use drop-down boxes.	☐ Yes!	☐ Not yet.
. . . use radio buttons.	☐ Yes!	☐ Not yet.

How Much Is It?

8.1 Vocabulary

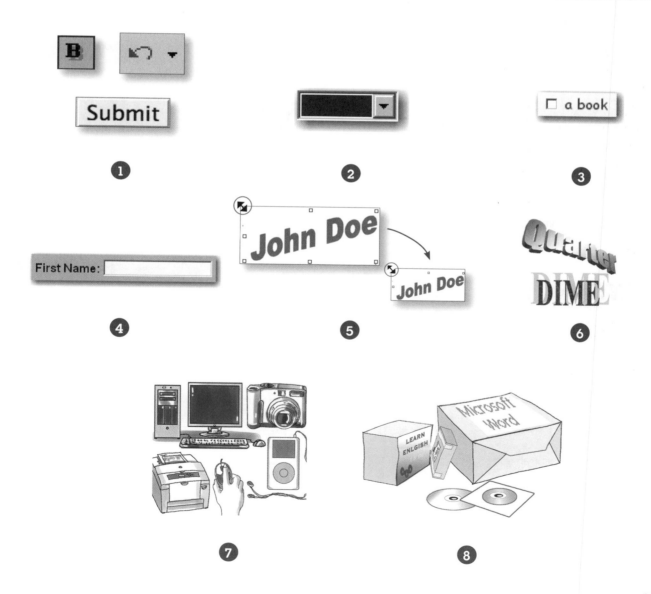

1 Submit

2

3 ☐ a book

4 First Name:

5 John Doe → John Doe

6 Quarter DIME

7

8 LEARN ENLGISH / Microsoft Word

Cyrus

8.2 Speaking

PARTNER A: *Look at page 101.*

PARTNER B: *Look at page 102. Say the words.*

PARTNER A: *Point to the picture.*

Change roles and repeat.

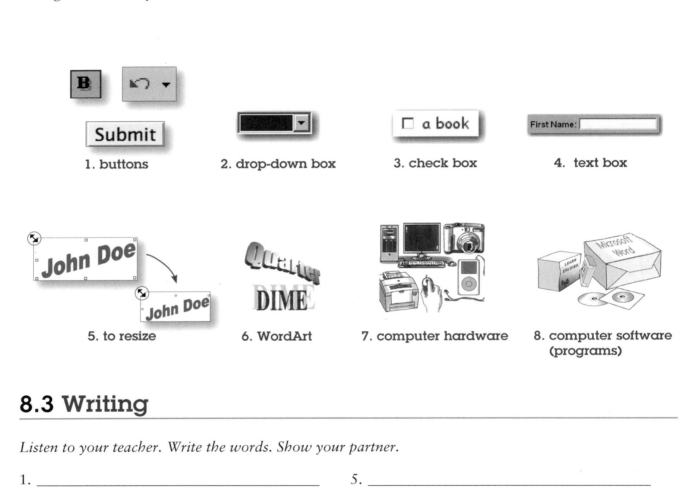

1. buttons   2. drop-down box   3. check box   4. text box

5. to resize   6. WordArt   7. computer hardware   8. computer software (programs)

8.3 Writing

Listen to your teacher. Write the words. Show your partner.

1. _____

2. _____

3. _____

4. _____

5. _____

6. _____

7. _____

8. _____

! IMPORTANT . . .

Stand up and stretch every 20 minutes.

8.4 Review

Aligning Words

1. Open Microsoft Word .

2. Save your document as **yourname.8.4.review** 💾 .

3. Type your name at the top.

4. Type the date.

5. Type your teacher's name.

Example:

> John Doe
> June 15, 2005
> Instructor: Tina Sander

6. Align your name to the right:

 • Highlight your name.

 • Click ▤ .

Example:

> ⟶ John Doe
> June 15, 2005
> Instructor: Tina Sander

7. Align the date to the right ▤ .

8. Align your teacher's name to the right ▤ .

9. Save 💾 .

Example:

> John Doe
> June 15, 2005
> ⟶ Instructor: Tina Sander

Copying and Pasting

1. Continue working in the document **yourname.8.4.review.**

2. Type:

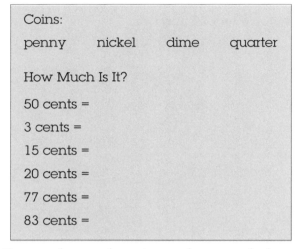

> Coins:
>
> penny   nickel   dime   quarter
>
> How Much Is It?
>
> 50 cents =
> 3 cents =
> 15 cents =
> 20 cents =
> 77 cents =
> 83 cents =

3. Copy and paste the coin words to match the number of cents.

Example:

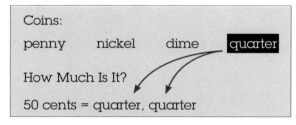

> Coins:
>
> penny   nickel   dime   **quarter**
>
> How Much Is It?
>
> 50 cents = quarter, quarter

4. Format the words. Use underline, bold, and italics.

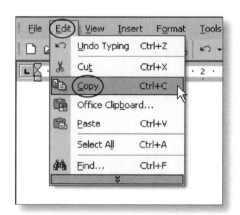

5. Center **Coins:**

   • Highlight **Coins.**

   • Click  .

Example:

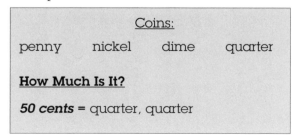

> <u>Coins:</u>
>
> penny   nickel   dime   quarter
>
> **How Much Is It?**
>
> ***50 cents*** = quarter, quarter

6. Save .

7. Close Microsoft Word .

8.5 Using WordArt

Inserting and Aligning WordArt

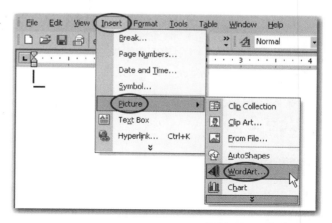

1. Open Microsoft Word 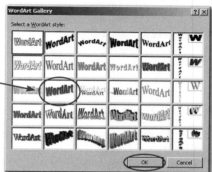.

2. Save the document as **yourname.8.5.wordart** .

3. Insert your name using WordArt:

   - Click **Insert**.
   - Click **Picture**.
   - Click **WordArt** .
   - Click on a style.
   - Click **OK**.
   - Type **your name**.
   - Click **OK**.
   - Click .
   - Press **Enter**.

Practice 1

4. Repeat step 3 to insert the date and your teacher's name using WordArt.

   Example:

5. Save .

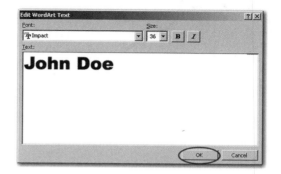

Resizing WordArt

6. Make your name smaller:

- Click on **your name**.
- Click and move a corner of the box.
- Click on white space.

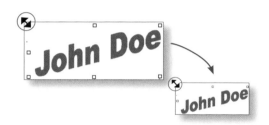

Practice 2

7. Repeat step 6 to make the date and your teacher's name smaller.

Practice 3

8. Complete these sentences:

I am from _____.

I like to shop at _____.

I like to eat _____.

9. Continue working with the document **yourname.8.5.wordart**.

10. Insert each sentence using WordArt:

- Click **Insert**.
- Click **Picture**.
- Click **WordArt** .
- Click on a style.
- Click **OK**.
- Type your sentence.
- Click **OK**.
- Click ▤.
- Press **Enter**.

11. Save 🖫.

12. Print 🖨.

13. Show your partner.

14. Close Microsoft Word ✖.

Example:

8.6 The Internet: Searching for Images

Before You Start

Ask four classmates:

> *What's your name?*
>
> *Where are you from?*
>
> *What money do you use in your native country?*

Write the answers:

Name	Country	Money
Yukiko	Japan	Yen

Searching for Images

1. Connect to the Internet 🅮 .

2. Open the Web site: www.google.com.

3. Click **Images**.

4. Type the money name.
   (Example: Mexican peso)

5. Click **Search Images** .

6. How many images are there? _____

7. Click on an image. Click on the image again.

8. Write the Web address:

   _____

9. Show your partner.

10. Click **← Back** two times. Show your partner.

11. Ask your partner:

    What are three traditional gifts in
    your country?

    _____

    _____

    _____

12. Find images of the three gifts.

13. Show your partner.

14. Disconnect from the Internet **✕** .

8.7 The Internet: Searching

1. Connect to the Internet 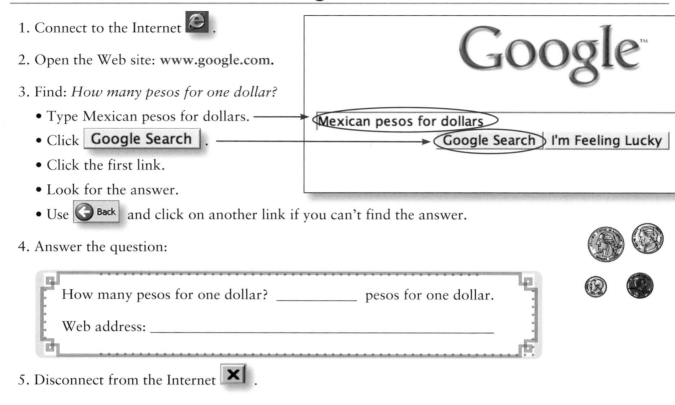.

2. Open the Web site: www.google.com.

3. Find: *How many pesos for one dollar?*

   • Type Mexican pesos for dollars. ⟶ Mexican pesos for dollars

   • Click Google Search . ⟶ Google Search I'm Feeling Lucky

   • Click the first link.

   • Look for the answer.

   • Use ← Back and click on another link if you can't find the answer.

4. Answer the question:

   > How many pesos for one dollar? _____ pesos for one dollar.
   >
   > Web address: _____

5. Disconnect from the Internet ✕ .

8.8 The Internet: Review

Using Drop-down Boxes

1. Connect to the Internet 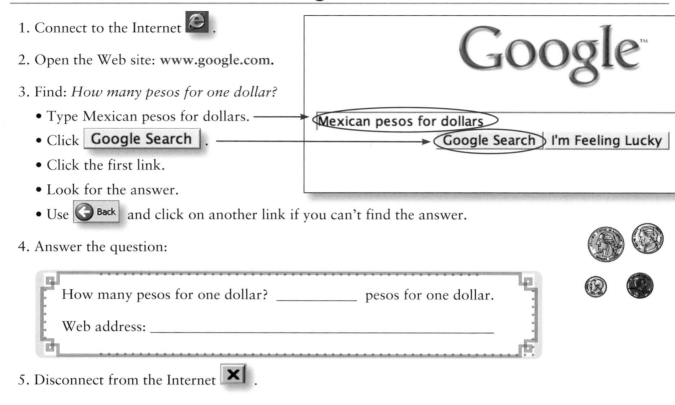.

2. Open the Web site: www.outandaboutenglish.com.

3. Click on **Unit 8**.

4. Click on **How much is it?**

5. Click the drop-down boxes. Answer the questions:

   • Click ▼ .

   • Click the answer.

   1. 5 nickels and 4 quarters =

   Select the answer ▼ .
   Select the answer
   35 cents
   90 cents
   $1.25

6. Click **Submit** .

7. Are your answers correct? Show your partner. Correct your answers.

8. Disconnect from the Internet ✕ .

8.9 The Internet: Using Check Boxes

1. Connect to the Internet 🌐 .

2. Open the Web site: www.outandaboutenglish.com.

3. Click on **Unit 8**.

4. Click on **What can you buy?**

5. Read the questions.

6. Answer the questions. Click the check boxes.

7. Click **Submit** .

8. Are your answers correct? Show your partner. Correct your answers.

9. Disconnect from the Internet ❌ .

> **You have $65.00 What can you buy for the kitchen?**
>
> ☑ a box of cereal ($4.50)
> ☐ a can of soup ($1.29)
> ☐ a bag of rice ($3.49)
> ☑ a gallon of milk ($4.29)
> ☑ a microwave ($79.99)
> ☐ a refrigerator ($499.99)
>
> (Submit)

8.10 The Internet: Using Text Boxes

Before You Start

Write the information:

Name: _____	Gender: ☐ male ☐ female
Address: _____	Children: ☐ yes ☐ no
_____	Native country: _____
Birthday: _____	Job: _____

Using Text Boxes

1. Connect to the Internet 🌐 .

2. Open the Web site:
   www.outandaboutenglish.com.

3. Click on **Unit 8**.

4. Click on **Personal Information**.

5. Fill out the form:
   - Click in the text boxes.
   - Type your information.
   - Use the drop-down boxes.
   - Click the radio buttons.

6. Click **Submit** .

7. Show your partner.

8. Disconnect from the Internet ❌ .

8.11 My Portfolio: A Flyer About Me

1. Open Microsoft Word 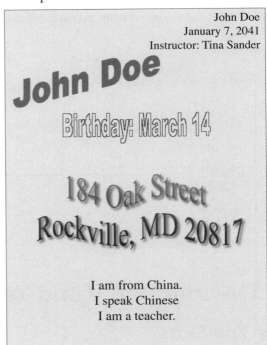.

2. Save the document as **yourname.8.11.aboutme.**

3. Type a heading with your name, the date, and your teacher's name

4. Align it to the right.

5. Use WordArt to make a flyer with your personal information.

6. Save.

7. Print.

8. Add this page to your portfolio.

9. Close Microsoft Word.

Example:

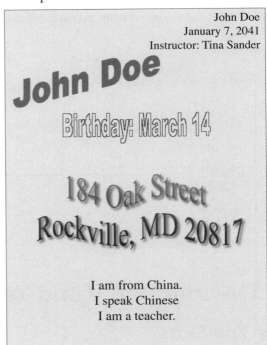

John Doe
January 7, 2041
Instructor: Tina Sander

John Doe

Birthday: March 14

184 Oak Street Rockville, MD 20817

I am from China.
I speak Chinese
I am a teacher.

8.12 The Internet: Restaurants

1. Connect to the Internet.

2. Open the Web site: **www.outandaboutenglish.com.**

3. Click on **Unit 8.**

4. Click on **Restaurant Menu.**

5. Read the menu.

6. Write three foods and their prices in the box below.

7. Show your partner.

8. Disconnect from the Internet.

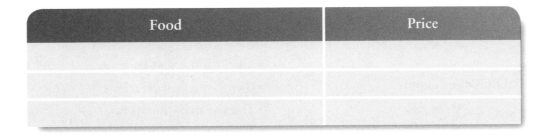

Food	Price

8.13 My Portfolio: A Party Invitation

Before You Start

Read the party invitation. Write the answers:

You're invited...

...to John's 50th birthday party!

When: Saturday, July 16ᵗʰ
6 p.m. to 10 p.m.

Where: Café Caroline
449 Prospect St.
Brooklyn, NY

For soups, salads, appetizers, sandwiches, and drinks!

RSVP Kate at 415-555-9093

A Party Invitation

a. When is the party? _____

b. Where is the party? _____

c. Is the party at a house or a restaurant?

_____

d. What kind of party is it?

_____

e. What does RSVP mean?

_____

f. Who is Kate? _____

A Party Invitation

1. Plan a party.
   Answer the questions.

2. Open Microsoft Word 🅆 .

3. Save the document as
   yourname.8.13.partyinvitation.

4. Use WordArt to make your
   party invitation.

5. Save 💾 .

6. Print your invitation 🖨 .

7. Show your partner the invitation.

8. Add this page to your portfolio.

9. Close Microsoft Word ❎ .

My Party

a. What day is your party? _____

b. What time is your party? _____

c. Where is the party? _____

d. What is the occasion? _____

8.14 My Portfolio: A Restaurant Advertisement

Before You Start

1. Answer these questions. →

2. Connect to the Internet .

3. Open the restaurant's Web site.

4. Find a link to the restaurant's menu.

5. Write three foods and their prices:

A Restaurant

a. What state/province do you live in? _____

b. What city do you live in? _____

c. What is the name of a restaurant in your city? _____

d. Find the Web address of the restaurant: _____

Food	Price

6. Disconnect from the Internet ☒.

A Restaurant Advertisement

1. Open Microsoft Word 𝖂.

2. Save the document as **yourname.8.15.restaurantadvertisement.**

3. Use WordArt to make an advertisement for the restaurant.

4. Save 💾.

5. Print 🖨.

6. Add this page to your portfolio.

7. Close Microsoft Word ☒.

Example:

Sunshine Bakery

coffee
tea
hot chocolate
Italian sodas
sandwiches
salads
homemade breads
desserts

Dine in or take out!

Open every day from 7 a.m. to 3 p.m.

1265 Main Street, Scotts Valley, CA 95066

8.15 Homework

The Internet: My Friends' Favorite Restaurants

1. Ask three friends: Where do you like to eat?

2. Write their answers:

Name of Friend	Name of Restaurant	City

3. Connect to the Internet 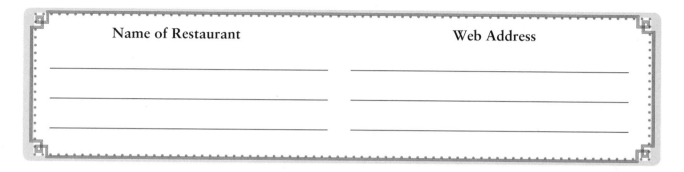.

4. Open the Web site: **www.google.com.**

5. Find one of your friends' restaurants:

- Type the name of the restaurant and the city.
- Click **Google Search** .
- Click the first link.
- Does the restaurant have a Web site? Look for the Web address.
- Use **Back** and click another link if you can't find the restaurant's Web address.

6. Write the Web address of the restaurant (if the restaurant does not have a Web site, write "no Web address"):

7. Repeat steps 3-4 for the other two restaurants.

8. Disconnect from the Internet .

9. Open Microsoft Word .

10. Save the document as **yourname.8.15.friendsrestaurants** .

11. Insert the restaurant names and Web addresses using WordArt.

12. Save .

13. Close Microsoft Word .

Name of Restaurant	Web Address

Unit 8 End-of-Unit Checklist

REVIEW		
I can . . .		
. . . align words to the right, left, and center.	☐ Yes!	☐ Not yet.
. . . copy and paste.	☐ Yes!	☐ Not yet.
. . . follow image and word links.	☐ Yes!	☐ Not yet.
. . . search for images on the Internet.	☐ Yes!	☐ Not yet.
. . . use www.google.com to find information.	☐ Yes!	☐ Not yet.
. . . use drop-down boxes.	☐ Yes!	☐ Not yet.
UNIT 8		
I can . . .		
. . . insert WordArt.	☐ Yes!	☐ Not yet.
. . . align WordArt.	☐ Yes!	☐ Not yet.
. . . resize WordArt.	☐ Yes!	☐ Not yet.
. . . search the Internet.	☐ Yes!	☐ Not yet.
. . . use check boxes.	☐ Yes!	☐ Not yet.
. . . use text boxes.	☐ Yes!	☐ Not yet.

What Are You Wearing?

9.1 Vocabulary

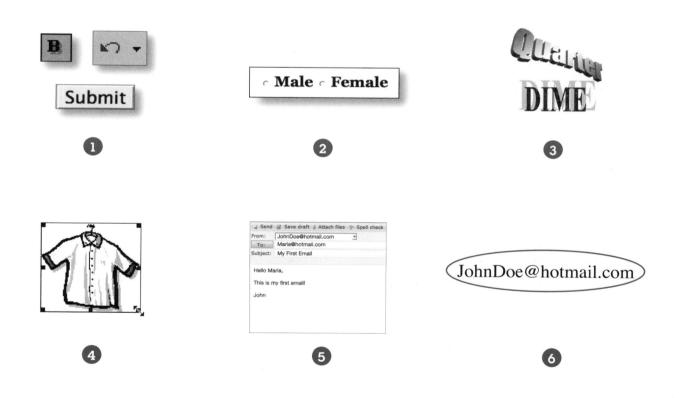

9.2 Speaking

PARTNER A: *Look at page 115.*

PARTNER B: *Look at page 116. Say the words.*

PARTNER A: *Point to the picture.*

Change roles and repeat.

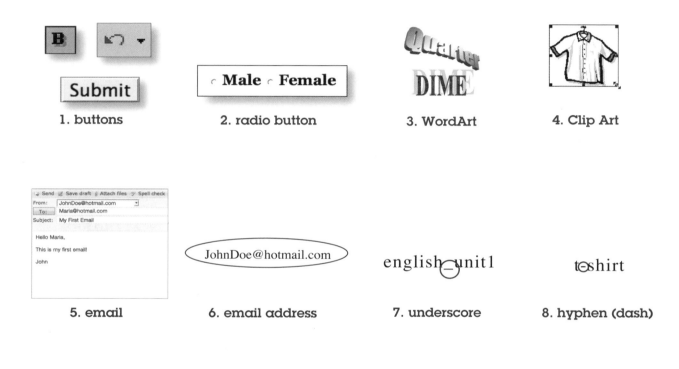

1. buttons   2. radio button   3. WordArt   4. Clip Art

5. email   6. email address   7. underscore   8. hyphen (dash)

9.3 Writing

Listen to your teacher. Write the words. Show your partner.

1. _____   5. _____

2. _____   6. _____

3. _____   7. _____

4. _____   8. _____

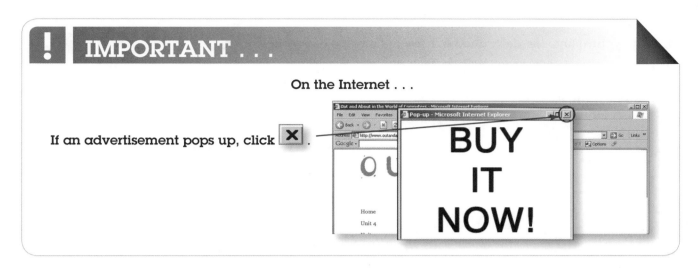

> **!** **IMPORTANT . . .**
>
> On the Internet . . .
>
> If an advertisement pops up, click **X** .

9.4 Review

Before You Start

Ask your partner: What are you wearing today? Write four sentences.

Example:

    A. *Rosaura, what are you wearing today?*
    B. *I am wearing a white shirt.*

Clothing

1. Rosaura is wearing a white shirt. _____

2. _____

3. _____

4. _____

5. _____

Aligning Words

1. Open Microsoft Word  .

2. Save the document as **yourname.9.4.review** 💾 .

3. Type a heading with your name, the date, and your teacher's name.

4. Align your name, the date, and your teacher's name to the right .

5. Type the title: **Clothing**.

6. Center **Clothing** .

Example:

> John Doe
> February 7, 2035
> Instructor: Tina Sander
>
> Clothing

7. Save .

Inserting a Table

1. Continue working with the document **yourname.9.4.review.**

2. Create a table with two columns and four rows.

3. Type **Sentences** and **Pictures** in the first row.

4. Format the words. Use bold and italics.

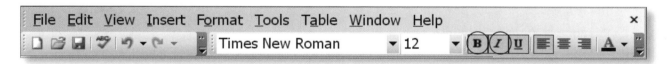

Example:

> John Doe
> February 7, 2035
> Instructor: Tina Sander
>
> **Clothing**

Sentences	*Pictures*

Using WordArt

1. Position the cursor in the second cell of the first column of your table.

2. Click **Insert**.

3. Click **Picture**.

4. Click **WordArt**.

5. Click a style.

6. Click **OK**.

7. Click and type a sentence about what your partner is wearing.

8. Click **OK**.

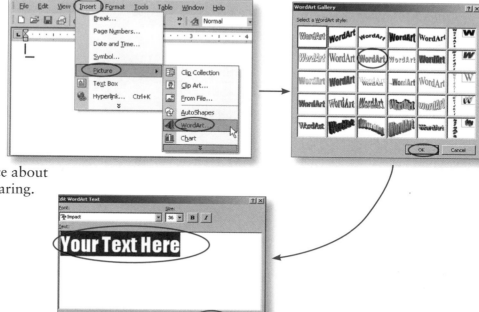

Resizing WordArt

9. Make your WordArt smaller:
   - Click on the WordArt.
   - Click and move a corner of the box.
   - Click on white space.

10. Save 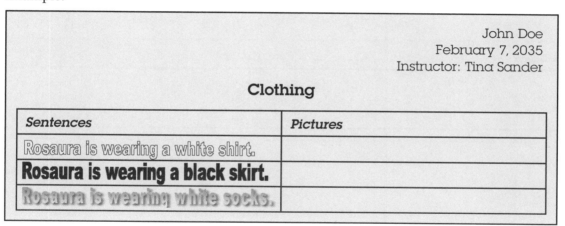.

11. Repeat steps 1–10 with two more sentences.

12. Close Microsoft Word.

Example:

<table>
<tr><td colspan="2" align="right">John Doe
February 7, 2035
Instructor: Tina Sander</td></tr>
<tr><td colspan="2" align="center">**Clothing**</td></tr>
<tr><td>*Sentences*</td><td>*Pictures*</td></tr>
<tr><td>Rosaura is wearing a white shirt.</td><td></td></tr>
<tr><td>**Rosaura is wearing a black skirt.**</td><td></td></tr>
<tr><td>Rosaura is wearing white socks.</td><td></td></tr>
</table>

9.5 Using Clip Art

Inserting Clip Art

1. Open Microsoft Word .

2. Open **yourname.9.4.review**.

3. Insert a Clip Art picture of the clothing item in your first sentence:

   - Position the cursor in the second cell of the second column in your table.
   - Click **Insert**.
   - Click **Picture**.
   - Click **Clip Art**.
   - Type the **clothing word** in the search text box.
   - Click **Search.**
   - Double-click a picture to insert.

Resizing Clip Art

4. Make your picture smaller:
   - Click on the picture.
   - Click and move a corner of the picture.

Practice 1

5. Repeat steps 3–4 to insert two more Clip Art pictures.

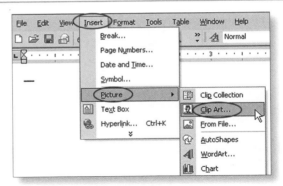

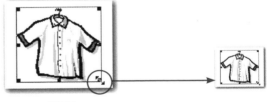

6. Save save .

7. Close Microsoft Word .

Example:

John Doe
February 7, 2035
Instructor: Tina Sander

Clothing

Sentences	Pictures
Rosaura is wearing a white shirt.	

Note to the Teacher: In some versions of Microsoft Word, students need to click Go (not Search) and they may need to click only once on a picture (not twice). See the online teacher's guide at www.outandaboutenglish.com for more information.

9.6 My Portfolio: My Home

1. Open Microsoft Word [W].

2. Save the document as **yourname.9.6.myhome** 💾.

3. Type a heading with your name, the date, and your teacher's name.

4. Align it to the right.

5. Insert the title **My Home** using WordArt ◢.

6. Center **My Home** ▤.

7. Press **Enter**.

8. Insert a Clip Art picture of a house:

- Click **Insert**.
- Click **Picture**.
- Click **Clip Art**.

- Type **home** in the search text box.
- Click **Search**.
- Double click a picture to insert.

9. Press **Enter** two times.

10. Type a paragraph about your home.

11. Align the paragraph to the left ▤.

12. Save 💾.

13. Print 🖨.

14. Add this page to your portfolio.

15. Close Microsoft Word ✖.

Example:

John Doe
March 1, 2035
Instructor: Tina Sander

My Home

I live in an apartment. It has one blue bedroom. It has a pink bathroom and a blue kitchen. There is a big table in the living room.

9.7 The Internet: Department Store Information

1. Connect to the Internet  .

2. Open the Web site: www.outandaboutenglish.com.

3. Click **Unit 9.**

4. Click **David's Department Store.**

5. Work with a partner. Click the word links to find store information.

6. Write your answers:

Click This Link	Question	Answer
	What does David's Department Store sell?	
Specials	What's on sale?	
	Where is David's Department Store?	
Employment	What job openings does David's Department Store have?	
	What is the Arizona store's telephone number and address?	
About Us	What hours are they open?	

7. Write a paragraph about David's Department Store:

_____

_____

_____

_____

_____

8. Show your paragraph to your partner.

9. Disconnect from the Internet ✕ .

9.8 The Internet: Department Store Specials

1. Connect to the Internet 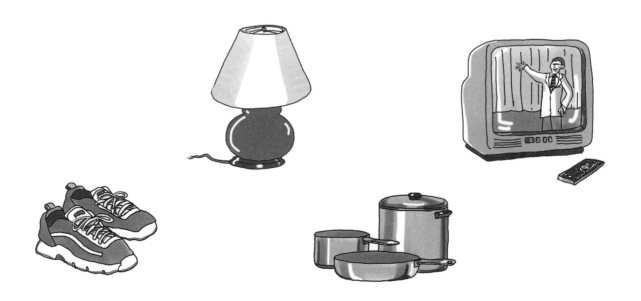.

2. Open the Web site www.outandaboutenglish.com.

3. Click **Unit 9**.

4. Click **David's Department Store**.

5. Click **Specials**.

6. Write the missing information:

What's on sale?	Where are they?	When does the sale end?	Other Information
children's shoes			
			The lamps come in different colors.
		March 22	
	In the electronics department		

7. Disconnect from the Internet ☒ .

9.9 The Internet: Finding a Job

1. Connect to the Internet  .

2. Open the Web site: www.outandaboutenglish.com.

3. Click **Unit 9.**

4. Click **David's Department Store.**

5. Click **Employment** to find job information.

6. Write your answers:

What is the job?	What does this person do?	Who can you call?	What are the hours?	What is the pay?
cashier				
				$10.00/hour
		Mike	Mon.—Fri. 10 a.m. to 2 p.m.	

7. Read the table and talk to your partner. Ask and answer the questions:

   a. What job do you want? (Cashier/Custodian/Telephone Receptionist/Gift Wrapper)

   _____

   b. Why do you want this job?

   _____

8. Disconnect from the Internet ☒ .

9.10 The Internet: Review

Searching for Images

1. Connect to the Internet .

2. Open the Web site: www.google.com.

3. Click Images.

4. Search for these clothing items. Write the information:

Clothing	Number of Images	What do they look like?
socks		
hat		
coat		

5. Show your partner.

6. Disconnect from the Internet [X].

9.11 The Internet: A Department Store Web Site

1. Connect to the Internet [e].

2. Open the Web site: www.google.com.

3. Type **Department Store,** the name of your city, and your state/province.

4. Click **Google Search**.

5. Find a department store Web site.

6. Use [Back] if necessary.

7. Open the Web site.

8. Write your answers in the form. →

9. Disconnect from the Internet [X].

Department Store Name:

_____

Web Address: _____

Email Address: _____

Street Address: _____

_____
City   State   Zip Code

Phone Number: _____

Store Hours: _____

Specials: _____

Jobs: _____

9.12 The Internet: A Survey

1. Connect to the Internet 🖉 .

2. Open the Web site: www.outandaboutenglish.com.

3. Click **Unit 9**.

4. Click **Clothing Survey.**

5. Answer the questions.

6. Click **Submit** .

7. Write your answers:

My Answers

Favorite Color: _____

Shoe Size: _____

Favorite Clothing: _____

_____

Do I like shopping? _____

8. Ask your partner:

- What's your favorite color?
- What's your shoe size?
- What do you like to wear?
- Do you like shopping?

9. Write your partner's answers:

My Partner's Answers

Favorite Color: _____

Shoe Size: _____

Favorite Clothing: _____

_____

Does my partner like shopping? _____

10. Disconnect from the Internet ❌ .

9.13 Email: Setting Up an Email Account

Before You Start

What do you know about email? Write words:

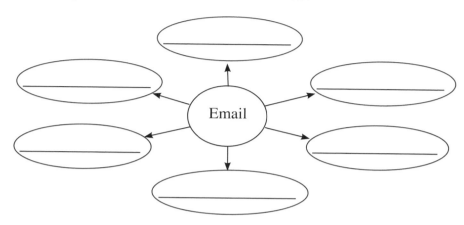

Your teacher will give you a form. Fill in the missing information.

Setting Up an Email Account

1. Listen to your teacher. Write the instructions:

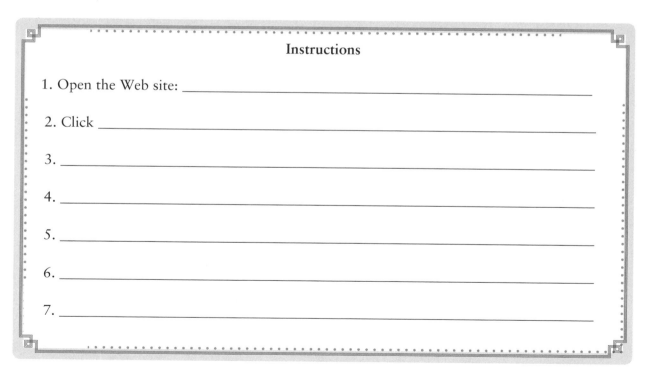

Instructions

1. Open the Web site: _____

2. Click _____

3. _____

4. _____

5. _____

6. _____

7. _____

Note to the Teacher: The form for this activity can be found in the online teacher's guide at www.outandaboutenglish.com.

2. Connect to the Internet  .

3. Sign up for an email account. Use the instructions on page 127.

> **My Email Account**
>
> My email address: _____
>
> My password: _____
>
> My secret question: _____
>
> My secret answer: _____

4. Disconnect from the Internet ❌ .

9.14 Email: Signing In to and Out of Your Email Account

Before You Start

Write your email address: _____

Write your password: _____

Signing In to and Out of Your Email Account

1. Connect to the Internet  .

2. Open the Web site: www.hotmail.com.

3. Type your email address in the text box.

4. Type your password in the text box.

5. Click **Sign in.**

6. Click **Sign out.**

9.15 Email: Reading Emails

1. Connect to the Internet  .

2. Open the Web site: www.hotmail.com.

3. Type your email address in the text box.

4. Type your password in the text box.

5. Click **Sign in.**

6. Click **Inbox.**

7. How many emails do you have? _____

8. Click an email.

9. Read the message.

10. Click **Sign out.**

11. Disconnect from the Internet  .

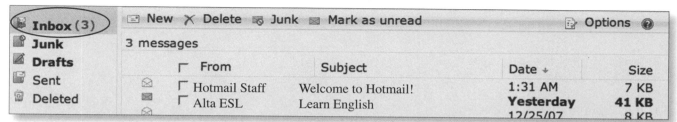

9.16 Email: Sending Emails

Before You Start

Ask six classmates: What's your email address? Write their information:

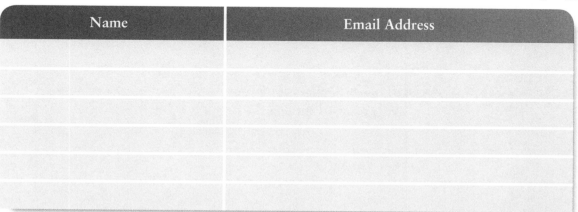

Name	Email Address

Sending an Email

1. Connect to the Internet 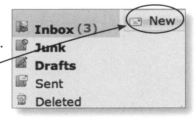 .

2. Open the Web site www.hotmail.com.

3. Type your email address in the text box.

4. Type your password in the text box.

5. Click **Sign in.**

6. Click **New.**

7. In the **To** text box, type a classmate's email address.

8. In the **Subject** text box, type **My First Email.**

9. In the **big text box,** type a message to your classmate.

10. Click **Send.**

11. Click **Sign out.**

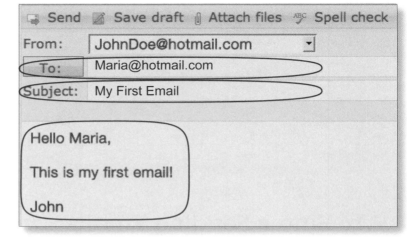

9.17 Email: Writing Emails

Before You Start

Write 3 sentences about your favorite clothing:

My Favorite Clothing

1. _____

2. _____

3. _____

Ask your partner: What's your email address?

Write your partner's email address: _____

Writing Emails

1. Connect to the Internet 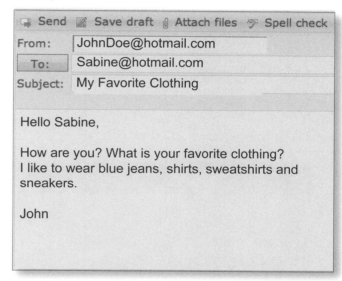.

2. Open the Web site: www.hotmail.com.

3. Sign in to your email account.

4. Send an email to your partner:

   - Click [✉ **New**].

   - In the **To** text box, type your partner's email address.

   - In the **Subject** text box, type **My Favorite Clothing**.

   - In the **big text box**, type a message to your partner.

5. Click **Send**.

6. Click **Sign out**.

Practice

1. Sign in to your email account.

2. Click **Inbox**.

3. Click your partner's email.

4. Read your partner's email.

5. Send emails to three other classmates. (Use the email addresses from **activity 9.16**.)

6. Click **Sign out**.

7. Disconnect from the Internet [✖].

Example:

⊟ Send ▨ Save draft ⬚ Attach files ᴬᴮᶜ Spell check

From: JohnDoe@hotmail.com

To: Sabine@hotmail.com

Subject: My Favorite Clothing

Hello Sabine,

How are you? What is your favorite clothing?
I like to wear blue jeans, shirts, sweatshirts and sneakers.

John

9.18 Homework

The Internet: A Supermarket

1. Connect to the Internet  .

2. Open the Web site: www.google.com.

3. Type **Supermarket,** the name of your city, and your state/province.

4. Click **Google Search** .

5. Find a supermarket Web site.

6. Use **Back** if necessary.

7. Open the Web site.

8. Write the Web address: _____

9. Write four specials and their prices:

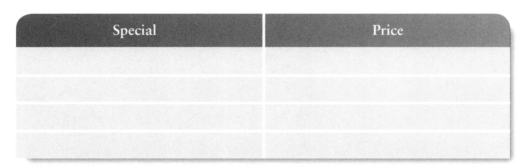

Special	Price

10. Find an email address for the supermarket: _____

11. Disconnect from the Internet ❎ .

corn 3/$1.00

Email: Friends and Family

1. Ask your friends and family for their email addresses.

2. Write their email addresses:

Name	Email Address

3. Connect to the Internet  .

4. Open the Web site: www.hotmail.com.

5. Sign in to your email account.

6. Send emails to your friends and family.

7. Click **Sign out**.

8. Disconnect from the Internet ☒ .

Example:

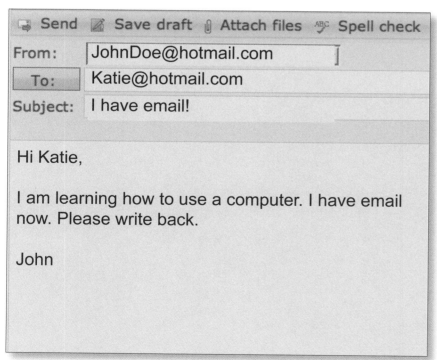

🖂 Send	📝 Save draft	📎 Attach files	🔤 Spell check
From:	JohnDoe@hotmail.com		
To:	Katie@hotmail.com		
Subject:	I have email!		

Hi Katie,

I am learning how to use a computer. I have email now. Please write back.

John

Unit 9 End-of-Unit Checklist

REVIEW		
I can . . .		
. . . align words to the right, left, and center.	☐ Yes!	☐ Not yet.
. . . insert tables.	☐ Yes!	☐ Not yet.
. . . use WordArt.	☐ Yes!	☐ Not yet.
. . . follow image and word links.	☐ Yes!	☐ Not yet.
. . . search for images on the Internet.	☐ Yes!	☐ Not yet.
. . . search the Internet.	☐ Yes!	☐ Not yet.
. . . use drop-down boxes, text boxes, check boxes, and radio buttons.	☐ Yes!	☐ Not yet.
UNIT 9		
I can . . .		
. . . insert Clip Art.	☐ Yes!	☐ Not yet.
. . . resize Clip Art.	☐ Yes!	☐ Not yet.
. . . set up an email account.	☐ Yes!	☐ Not yet.
. . . sign in to my email account.	☐ Yes!	☐ Not yet.
. . . read an email.	☐ Yes!	☐ Not yet.
. . . send an email.	☐ Yes!	☐ Not yet.
. . . sign out of my email account.	☐ Yes!	☐ Not yet.

Places in the Community

10.1 Vocabulary

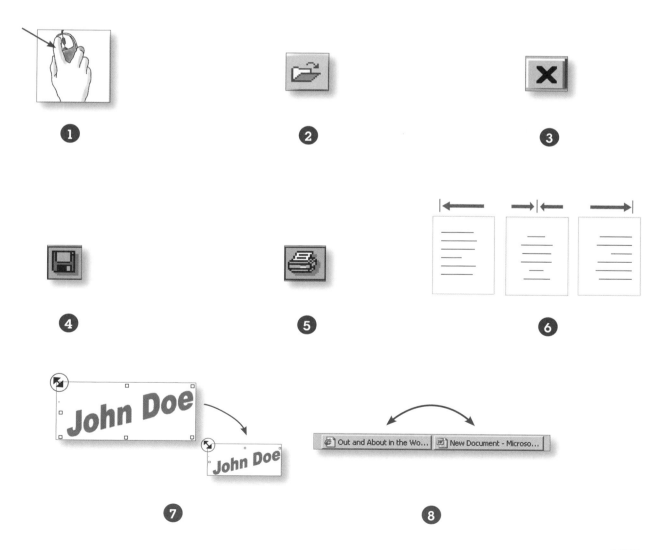

1

2

3

4

5

6

7

8

10.2 Speaking

PARTNER A: *Look at page 135.*

PARTNER B: *Look at page 136. Say the words.*

PARTNER A: *Point to the picture.*

Change roles and repeat.

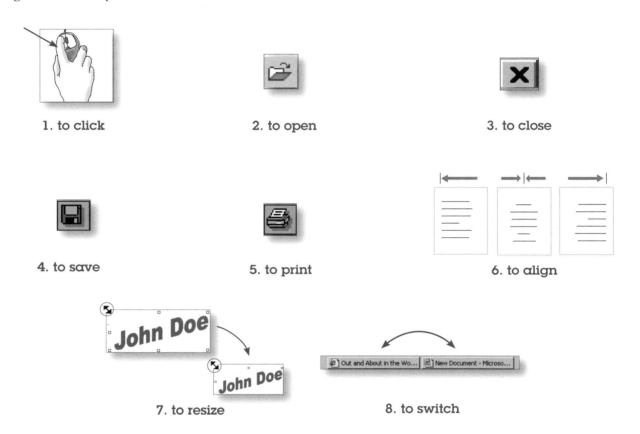

1. to click

2. to open

3. to close

4. to save

5. to print

6. to align

7. to resize

8. to switch

10.3 Writing

Listen to your teacher. Write the words. Show your partner.

1. _____

2. _____

3. _____

4. _____

5. _____

6. _____

7. _____

8. _____

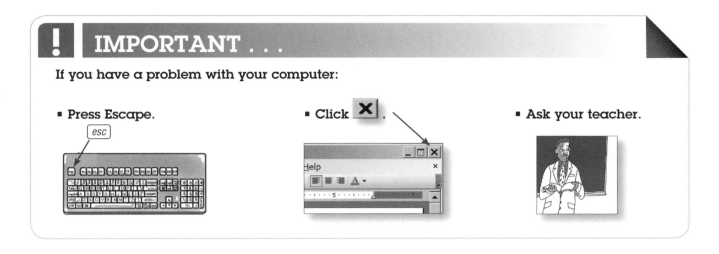

10.4 Review

Aligning and Formatting Words

1. Open Microsoft Word.

2. Save the document as **yourname.10.4.mycommunity**.

3. Type a heading with your name, the date, and your teacher's name.

4. Align your name, the date, and your teacher's name to the right.

5. Type the title: **My Community**.

6. Center **My Community**.

7. Type a paragraph about your community.

8. Align the paragraph to the left.

9. Indent the first word.

10. Format the words. Use bold, underline, and italics.

11. Save.

Example:

> *John Doe*
> *September 28, 2078*
> *Instructor: Tina Sander*
>
> <u>**My Community**</u>
>
>   I live in Santa Cruz, California. It is near San Francisco. We have good restaurants and shopping. The beaches are beautiful. I have a bank, a post office, a bookstore, a supermarket, a movie theater, and a park in my neighborhood.

Using WordArt

12. Use WordArt to type your city, your state or province, and your country after the paragraph.

13. Press **Enter**.

Using Clip Art

14. Insert a picture of the world:
    - Click **Insert**.
    - Click **Picture**.
    - Click **Clip Art**.
    - Type **world** in the search text box.
    - Click **Search**.
    - Double click a picture to insert.

15. Insert another Clip Art picture.

16. Save 💾 .

17. Close Microsoft Word ❌ .

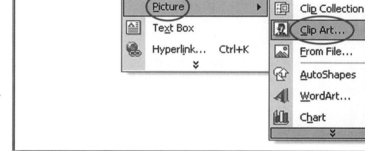

Example:

10.5 Inserting Footers

1. Open Microsoft Word 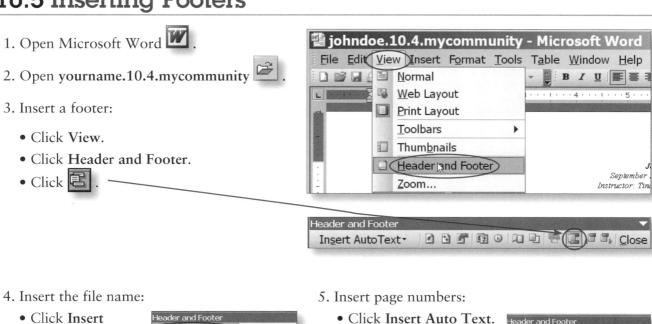.

2. Open **yourname.10.4.mycommunity** .

3. Insert a footer:

   • Click **View**.
   • Click **Header and Footer**.
   • Click .

4. Insert the file name:

   • Click **Insert AutoText**.
   • Click **Filename**.
   • Press **Tab**.

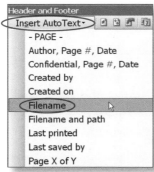

5. Insert page numbers:

   • Click **Insert Auto Text**.
   • Click **Page X of Y**.
   • Click **Close**.

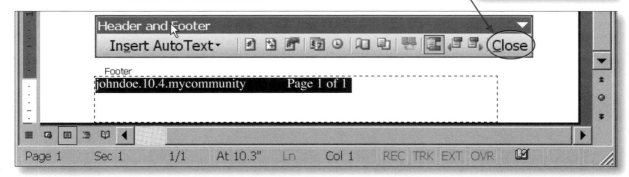

6. What is your file name? _____

7. How many pages does your document have? _____

8. Save .

9. Close Microsoft Word .

Practice

1. Open Microsoft Word 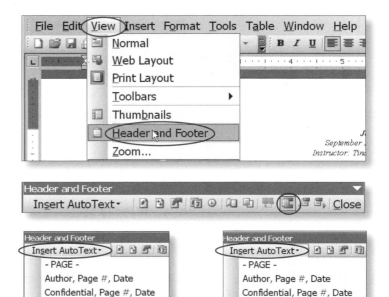.

2. Open **yourname.9.4.review**.

3. Insert a footer:
   - Click **View**.
   - Click **Header and Footer**.
   - Click [icon].

4. Insert the file name:
   - Click **Insert Auto Text**.
   - Click **Filename**.

5. Insert page numbers:
   - Click **Insert Auto Text**.
   - Click **Page X of Y**.

6. Click **Close**.

7. Save [icon].

8. Close Microsoft Word [icon].

10.6 Switching Between the Internet and Microsoft Word

1. Connect to the Internet 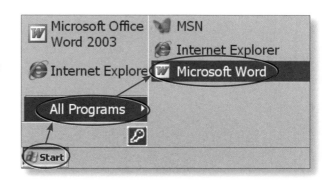.

2. Open the Web site: www.google.com.

3. **DO NOT** disconnect from the Internet.

4. Open Microsoft Word using the Start menu:
   - Click **Start**.
   - Click **All Programs**.
   - Click **Microsoft Word** [icon].

5. Open **yourname.10.4.mycommunity** .

Note to the teacher: The Microsoft Word button might read "Microsoft Office Word" depending on the version installed. See the online teacher's guide at www.outandaboutenglish.com for more information.

6. Switch to the Internet:

Click .

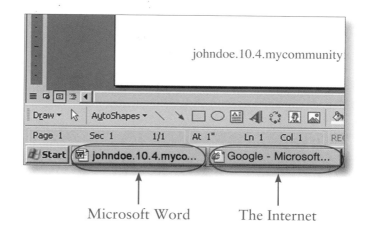

7. Switch to Microsoft Word:

Click .

8. Repeat steps 6 and 7 three times.

9. Close Microsoft Word .

10. Disconnect from the Internet .

Microsoft Word   The Internet

10.7 The Internet: Copying and Pasting Images

1. Use the Start menu to open Microsoft Word:

- Click **Start**.
- Click **All Programs**.
- Click **Microsoft Word** .

2. Open **yourname.10.4.mycommunity** .

3. Use the Start menu to connect to the Internet:

- Click **Start**.
- Click **All Programs**.
- Click **Internet Explorer** .

4. Open the Web site: www.google.com.

5. Find a picture of a place in your city:

- Click .
- Type the name of your city and state or province in the text box.
- Click .

6. Copy an image from the Web page:

- Right click an image.
- Left click **Copy**.

7. Paste the image into Microsoft Word:

- Click .
- Right click in the document.
- Left click **Paste**.
- Click on white space.

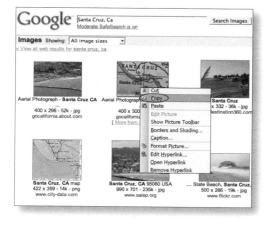

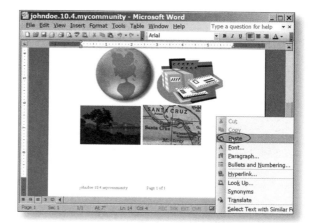

8. Make the image bigger or smaller:

- Click on the image.
- Click and move a corner of the image.

9. Press the space bar twice.

10. Save 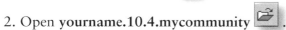.

11. Close Microsoft Word .

12. Disconnect from the Internet .

10.8 My Portfolio: My Community

1. Use the Start menu to open Microsoft Word:

- Click **Start**.
- Click **All Programs**.
- Click **Microsoft Word** .

2. Open **yourname.10.4.mycommunity** .

3. Use the Start menu to connect to the Internet:

- Click **Start**.
- Click **All Programs**.
- Click **Internet Explorer** .

4. Find one more image:

- Click Images .
- Type the name of your city and state or province in the text box.
- Click Search Images .

5. Copy an image from the Web page:

- Right click an image.
- Left click **Copy**.

6. Paste the image into Microsoft Word:

- Click johndoe.10.4.myco... .
- Right click in the document.
- Left click **Paste**.
- Click on white space.

7. Save .

8. Print .

Example:

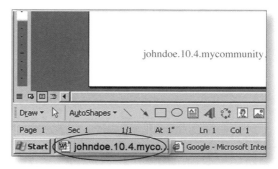

9. Add this page to your portfolio.

10. Close Microsoft Word .

11. Disconnect from the Internet .

10.9 My Portfolio: My Native Country

Before You Start

1. Open the Web site: www.outandaboutenglish.com.

2. Click **Unit 10**.

3. Click **In the USA**.

4. Read **The USA**.

5. Fill in the information:

	USA
Famous Person	Marilyn Monroe, famous actress, beautiful
Famous Place	
Traditional Clothing	
Popular Food	

6. Disconnect from the Internet ☒ .

7. Write about your native country:

	My Native Country
Famous Person	
Famous Place	
Traditional Clothing	
Popular Food	

8. Talk with your partner:

Tell me about a famous person in your native country.

Tell me about a famous place in your native country.

Tell me about traditional clothing in your native country.

Tell me about a popular food in your native country.

My Native Country

1. Use the Start menu to open Microsoft Word.

2. Save the document as **yourname.10.9.mynativecountry** .

3. Type a heading with your name, the date, and your teacher's name. Align it to the right .

4. Insert a footer.

5. Use WordArt to insert a title.

6. Create a table with two columns and four rows.

7. Save .

8. Use the Start menu to connect to the Internet .

9. Go to the Web site: **www.google.com**.

10. Find an image of a famous person from your native country.

11. Copy the image.

12. Paste the image into Microsoft Word.

13. Write about the image.

14. Name the image using WordArt.

15. Cut and paste images of a famous place, traditional clothing, and a popular food from your native country.

16. Repeat steps 12 and 13 for the three images.

17. Save .

18. Print .

19. Add this page to your portfolio.

20. Close Microsoft Word .

21. Disconnect from the Internet .

Example:

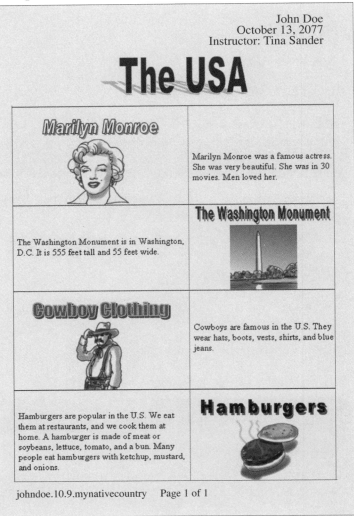

10.10 The Internet: A Bookstore

1. Connect to the Internet  .

2. Open the Web site: www.outandaboutenglish.com.

3. Click **Unit 10**.

4. Click **A Bookstore**.

5. Answer the questions:

> **A Bookstore**
>
> a. How many books are there? _____
>
> b. What book did Mary Shelley write? _____
>
> c. Where can you buy *Hocus Pocus?* _____
>
> d. Who wrote *Romeo and Juliet?* _____
>
> e. How much is *The Old Man and the Sea?* _____
>
> f. Which book is the cheapest? _____
>
> g. Which book is the most expensive? _____

6. Write the information for two books:

Title	Author	Store	Price

7. Click **Order a Book**.

8. Complete the form:
   - Type your personal information.
   - Type the information from step 6.

9. Click Submit .

10. Write:

> Today's date _____
>
> Web address _____
>
> Order number _____

11. Disconnect from the Internet ☒ .

10.11 The Internet: Online Bookstores

1. Connect to the Internet  .

2. Open the Web site: www.outandaboutenglish.com.

3. Click **Unit 10.**

4. Click **A Bookstore.**

5. Click | Internet Bookstores | .

6. Click on the Web address links.

7. Find some books.

8. Write the information for three books:

Title	Author	Store	Price

9. Show your partner.

10. Disconnect from the Internet ☒ .

10.12 The Internet: The Library

1. Connect to the Internet 🅔 .

2. Open the Web site: www.google.com.

3. Find the Web address of your public library: _____

4. Find the following information. Write the answers:

> **My Public Library**
>
> Library name: _____
>
> Email address: _____
>
> Address: _____
>
> Phone number: _____ Hours: _____
>
> Events: _____
>
> One book title: _____

5. Disconnect from the Internet ☒ .

10.13 The Internet: The Post Office

1. Connect to the Internet .

2. Open the Web site: www.outandaboutenglish.com.

3. Click **Unit 10.**

4. Click **The Post Office.**

5. Read the Web page.

6. What can you do at the post office? Write the answers:

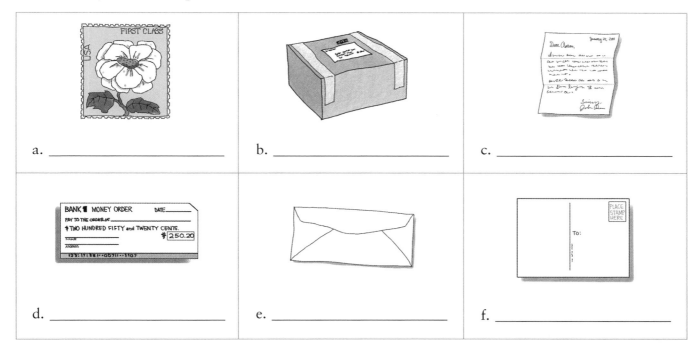

a. _____

b. _____

c. _____

d. _____

e. _____

f. _____

7. Click on the Web site link to the US Post Office.

8. What can you do on the US Post Office Web site?

US Post Office Web site		
Can you find a zip code?	☐ Yes	☐ No
Can you buy stamps?	☐ Yes	☐ No
Can you find a post office where you live?	☐ Yes	☐ No
Can you learn how much it costs to send a letter?	☐ Yes	☐ No

9. Disconnect from the Internet ☒ .

10.14 Email: Review

Signing In to Your Email Account

1. Connect to the Internet 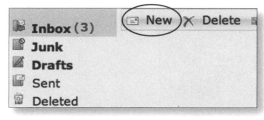.

2. Open the Web site: www.hotmail.com.

3. Type your email address and password in the text boxes.

4. Click **Sign In**.

Sending Emails

5. Send an email to your partner:

- Click ☐ **New**.

- In the **To** text box, type your partner's email address.

- In the **Subject** text box, type **My Community**.

- In the **big text box,** type a message to your partner.

- Click **Send**.

- Click **Sign out**.

Reading Emails

6. Sign in to your email account.

7. Click **Inbox**.

8. Click your partner's email.

9. Read the message.

10. Click **Sign out**.

11. Disconnect from the Internet ☒ .

10.15 Email: Replying to Emails

1. Connect to the Internet .

2. Open the Web site: **www.hotmail.com**.

3. Sign in to your email account.

4. Open and read an email from your partner.

5. Reply to your partner's email:

   - Click **Reply**.
   - Type a message about your neighborhood.
   - Click **Send**.

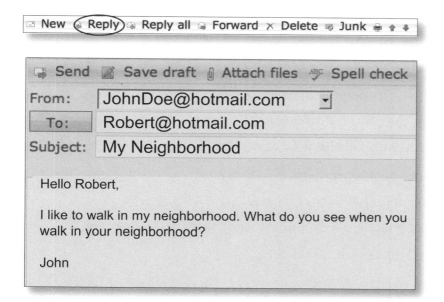

Practice

1. Read an email from your partner.

2. Reply to your partner's email.

3. Click **Sign out**.

4. Disconnect from the Internet ☒ .

10.16 My Portfolio: My Community Contacts

Before You Start

1. Use the Internet to find a laundromat in your neighborhood. Search for **Laundromat**, your city, and your state or province. What's the phone number?

_____

2. Find a post office in your neighborhood. What's the street address?

_____

3. Find a drugstore in your neighborhood. When is it open?

_____

My Community Contacts

1. Open Microsoft Word 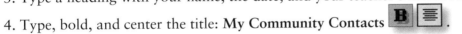.

2. Save the document as **yourname.10.16.communitycontacts** .

3. Type a heading with your name, the date, and your teacher's name. Align it to the right .

4. Type, bold, and center the title: **My Community Contacts** .

5. Insert a footer with the **file name** and **page X of Y**.

6. Make a table with six columns and four rows.

7. Type **Name, Address, Telephone Number, Web Address,** and **Hours** in the first row.

8. In the first column, type three places in your community.

Example:

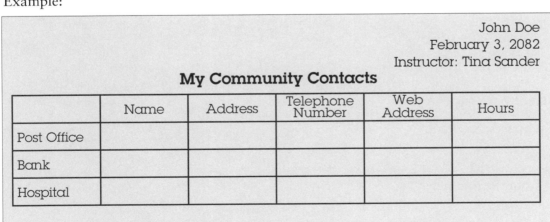

9. Complete your table with information from the Internet:

- Connect to the Internet .
- Go to the Web site: **www.google.com.**
- Search for the information.
- Type the information into your Microsoft Word table.

10. Save .

11. Print .

12. Add this page to your portfolio.

13. Close Microsoft Word **X** .

14. Disconnect from the Internet **X** .

10.17 Homework

The Internet: A Tourist Site in My Country

1. Use the Internet to find a tourist site in your country.

   What's the Web address?_____

2. Open Microsoft Word **W** .

3. Save the document as **yourname.10.17.touristsite** .

4. Type a heading with your name, the date, and your teacher's name. Align it to the right .

5. Type, bold, and center the title: **A Tourist Site in My Country** **B** .

6. Insert a footer with the **file name** and **page X of Y.**

7. Type a paragraph about the tourist site.

8. Save .

9. Close Microsoft Word **X** .

Unit 10 End-of-Unit Checklist

REVIEW		
I can . . .		
. . . align and format words.	☐ Yes!	☐ Not yet.
. . . use WordArt.	☐ Yes!	☐ Not yet.
. . . use Clip Art.	☐ Yes!	☐ Not yet.
. . . sign in to and out of my email account.	☐ Yes!	☐ Not yet.
. . . send emails.	☐ Yes!	☐ Not yet.
. . . read emails.	☐ Yes!	☐ Not yet.
UNIT 10		
I can . . .		
. . . insert footers in Microsoft Word documents.	☐ Yes!	☐ Not yet.
. . . use the Start menu to open Microsoft Word.	☐ Yes!	☐ Not yet.
. . . switch between the Internet and Microsoft Word.	☐ Yes!	☐ Not yet
. . . use the Start menu to connect to the Internet.	☐ Yes!	☐ Not yet.
. . . copy and paste images from the Internet.	☐ Yes!	☐ Not yet.
. . . reply to emails.	☐ Yes!	☐ Not yet.

UNIT 11

I'd Like to Make An Appointment.

11.1 Vocabulary

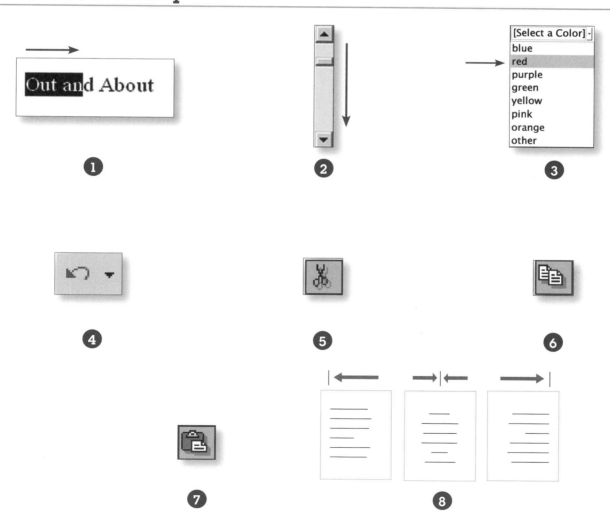

11.2 Speaking

PARTNER A: *Look at page 153.*

PARTNER B: *Look at page 154. Say the words.*

PARTNER A: *Point to the picture.*

Change roles and repeat.

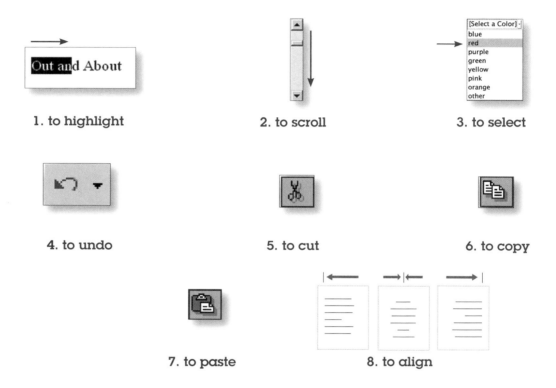

1. to highlight	2. to scroll	3. to select
4. to undo	5. to cut	6. to copy
7. to paste	8. to align	

11.3 Writing

Listen to your teacher. Write the words. Show your partner.

1. _____

2. _____

3. _____

4. _____

5. _____

6. _____

7. _____

8. _____

 **IMPORTANT . . .**

Use buttons when you can. Which buttons do you know?

11.4 Review

1. Open Microsoft Word .
2. Save the document as **yourname.11.4.bodyparts** .
3. Type a heading with your name, the date, and your teacher's name.
4. Align it to the right .
5. Type, bold, and center the title: **Body Parts** .
6. Insert a table with two columns and four rows.
7. Insert a footer with the file name and page numbers:

   - Click **View.**
   - Click **Header and Footer.**
   - Click .
   - Click **Insert AutoText.**
   - Click **Filename.**
   - Press **Tab.**
   - Click **Insert AutoText.**
   - Click **Page X of Y.**
   - Click **Close.**

Example:

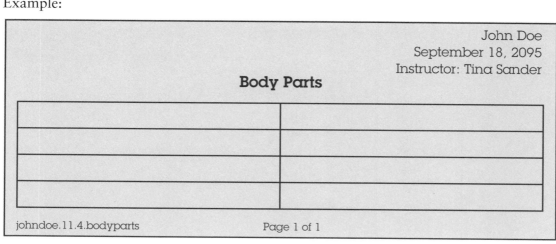

8. Use WordArt to insert these words in the first column:

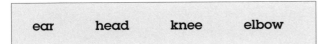

9. Insert a Clip Art picture of an ear in the second column.

10. Save .

11. Close Microsoft Word .

Example:

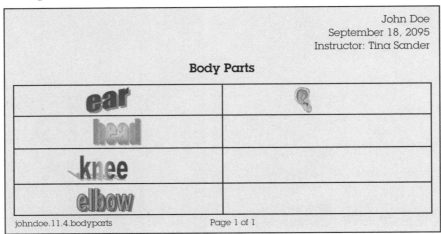

11.5 Inserting Borders

1. Open Microsoft Word 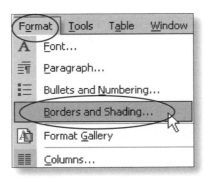.

2. Open **yourname.11.4.bodyparts** 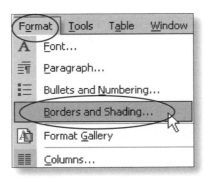.

4. Save 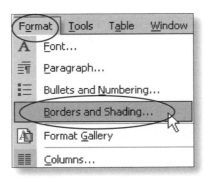.

5. Close Microsoft Word 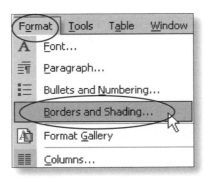.

3. Insert a border:

- Click **Format.**
- Click **Borders and Shading.**
- Click **Page Border.**
- Click **Box.**
- Select **Art** ▼.
- Click **OK.**

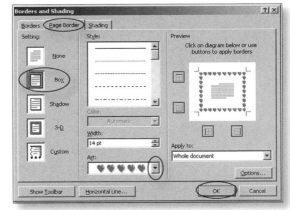

Example:

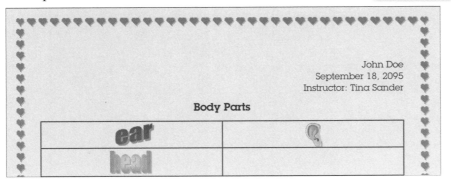

11.6 My Portfolio: Body Parts

1. Use the Start menu to connect to the Internet:

   - Click **Start**.
   - Click **All Programs**.
   - Click **Internet Explorer** 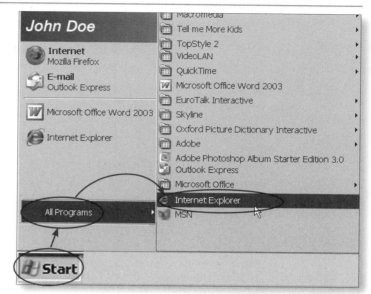 .

2. Copy an image of a person's head from the Internet:

   - Open the Web site: www.outandaboutenglish.com.
   - Click **Unit 11**.
   - Click **Review Body Parts**.
   - Find the image of a head.
   - Right click the image.
   - Left click **Copy**.

3. Use the Start menu to open Microsoft Word 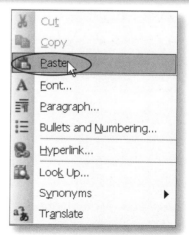 .

4. Open **yourname.11.4.bodyparts** .

5. Click in the second row of the second column.

6. Paste the image:

   - Right click.
   - Left click **Paste**.
   - Click on white space.

7. Resize the image (make the image bigger or smaller).

8. Save 💾 .

9. Repeat the steps to find images for **knee** and **elbow**.

10. Save 💾 .

11. Print 🖨 .

12. Add this page to your portfolio.

13. Close Microsoft Word ✖ .

14. Disconnect from the Internet ✖ .

Example:

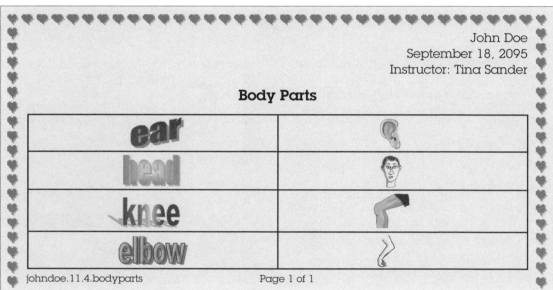

11.7 My Portfolio: The Cover Page

Before You Start

Look at the title page of this book. Write the answers:

My Computer Book

a. What is the title? _____

b. Who wrote the book? _____

c. Who is the publisher? _____

d. What year was the book published? _____

Answer these questions about your portfolio:

My Portfolio

a. What is the title of your portfolio? _____

b. Who is the author? _____

c. What is the name of your school? _____

d. What is today's date? _____

The Cover Page

1. Open Microsoft Word 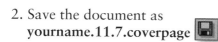 .

2. Save the document as **yourname.11.7.coverpage** 💾 .

Example:

3. Use Word Art to type the title **My Portfolio,** your name, and the name of your school.

4. Insert an image.

5. Insert a border:
   • Click **Format.**
   • Click **Borders and Shading.**
   • Click **Page Border.**
   • Click **Box.**
   • Select **Art** ▼ .
   • Click **OK.**

6. Save 💾 .

7. Print 🖨 .

8. Add this page to your portfolio.

9. Close Microsoft Word ✖ .

11.8 The Internet: What's the matter?

Before You Start

1. Connect to the Internet 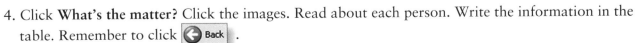 .

2. Open the Web site: www.outandaboutenglish.com.

3. Click **Unit 11.**

4. Click **What's the matter?** Click the images. Read about each person. Write the information in the table. Remember to click 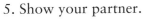 .

5. Show your partner.

Advice
Make an appointment with a doctor.
Make an appointment with a dentist.
Make an appointment with a hair stylist.
Eat ice cream and watch TV.
Go to sleep.
Take medicine.
Do nothing.
Eat soup.
Stay home.
Call a mechanic.
Call your mother.
Drink water.

Name	What's the matter?	What should he/she do?
Lance	Lance has a fever.	-drink water -eat soup -call his mother -go to sleep
David		
Catherine		
Greg		
Alex		
Abraham		

What's the matter?

1. Use the Start menu to Open Microsoft Word .

2. Save the document as **yourname.11.8.mybody** .

3. Type a paragraph about one person from the table on page 160.

4. Save .

5. Switch back to the Internet.

6. Copy and paste the picture of the person from the Web page into your Microsoft Word document.

7. Save .

Example:

> Lance is a student. He has a fever. He should go to sleep. He should drink water and eat soup. He should call his mother.

8. Close Microsoft Word .

9. Disconnect from the Internet .

11.9 The Internet: Copying and Pasting Words

1. Open Microsoft Word .

2. Save the document as **yourname.11.9.advice** .

3. Insert this table:

Name	Problem	Image: Body Part	What should I do?

4. Save .

5. Connect to the Internet .

6. Open the Web site: www.outandaboutenglish.com.

7. Click **Unit 11**.

8. Click **What should I do?**

9. Find three names and type them in the first column of the table.

Example:

Name	Problem	Image: Body Part	What should I do?
Rita			
Mari			
Joe			

10. Copy a problem word from the Web page and paste it into your Microsoft Word table:

- Highlight a problem word.
- Right click.
- Left click **Copy**.
- Switch to Microsoft Word .
- Click in the second column.
- Right click.
- Click **Paste**.
- Save .

11.9 The Internet: What should I do?

earache · toothache · sore knee · dizzy · arm · shoulder · foot · leg · stomach · knee

Show Picture
Save Picture As...
E-mail Picture...
Print Picture...
Go to My Pictures
Set as Background
Cut
Copy

Example:

Name	Problem	Image: Body Part	What should I do?
Rita	toothache		
Mari			
Joe			

11. Repeat step 10 two more times.

12. Copy three images from the Web page and paste them into your Microsoft Word document:

- Right click an image.
- Click **Copy**.
- Switch to Microsoft Word ![W] .
- Click in the third column.
- Right click.
- Click **Paste**.
- Click on white space.
- Save ![save] .

Example:

Name	Problem	Image: Body Part	What should I do?
Rita	toothache		

13. Repeat step 12 two more times.

14. What should I do? Type the answers in the fourth column.

Example:

Name	Problem	Image: Body Part	What should I do?
Rita	toothache		Make an appointment with a dentist.

15. Save ![save] .

16. Show your partner.

17. Close Microsoft Word ![X] .

18. Disconnect from the Internet ![X] .

11.10 The Internet: Copying and Pasting News Articles

1. Connect to the Internet .

2. Open the Web site: www.google.com.

3. Type the name of a newspaper from your country.

4. Click **Google Search** .

5. Open the newspaper's Web site.

6. Find and read an article.

7. Copy the article:
   - Highlight the article.
   - Right click.
   - Click **Copy**.

8. Use the Start menu to open Microsoft Word **W** .

9. Save the document as **yourname.11.10.news** .

10. Type a heading with your name, the date, and your teacher's name. Align it to the right .

11. Insert a footer with the file name and the page numbers.

12. Paste the newspaper article from the Internet into your Microsoft Word document:
    - Right click.
    - Click **Paste**.

13. Save .

14. Close Microsoft Word **X** .

15. Disconnect from the Internet **X** .

11.11 The Internet: Copying and Pasting Web Addresses

1. Connect to the Internet .

2. Go to the Web site of the Internet newspaper you found.

3. Copy the Web address from the Internet and paste it into your Microsoft Word document:
   - Highlight the Web address.
   - Right click.
   - Left click **Copy**.
   - Open Microsoft Word **W** .
   - Open **yourname.11.10.news** .
   - Right click.
   - Click **Paste**.
   - Save .

4. Close Microsoft Word **X** .

5. Disconnect from the Internet **X** .

Example:

> John Doe
> June 2, 2092
> Instructor: Tina Sander
>
> http://www.nytimes.com/2008/01/22/health/nutrition/22real.html
> ?_r=1&ref=health&oref=slogin
>
> **The Claim: Too Much Cola Can Cause Kidney Problems**
>
> Published: January 22, 2092
>
> It is well known that too much soda can increase the risk of diabetes and obesity. But when it comes to kidney problems, is there a difference between colas and other kinds of soda?
>
> johndoe.11.10.news   Page 1 of 1

11.12 Email: Review

Using Email

1. Connect to the Internet .

2. Go to the Web site: www.hotmail.com.

3. Sign in to your email account.

4. Send an email to your partner.

5. Read your partner's email.

6. Reply to your partner's email.

7. Click **Sign out.**

8. Disconnect from the Internet ☒ .

Example:

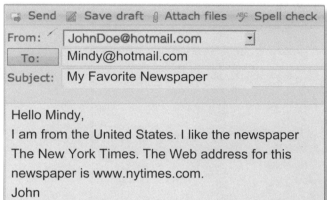

11.13 The Internet: The Refresh Button

1. Connect to the Internet .

2. Go to the Web site: www.hotmail.com.

3. Sign in to your email account.

4. Click **Inbox.**

5. Ask your partner to send you an email. (Say, "Please send me an email.")

6. Wait.

7. Can you see your partner's email? _____

8. Click Refresh ⟳ .

9. Can you see your partner's email now? _____

10. Click **Sign out.**

11. Disconnect from the Internet ☒ .

11.14 Email: Deleting Emails

1. Connect to the Internet 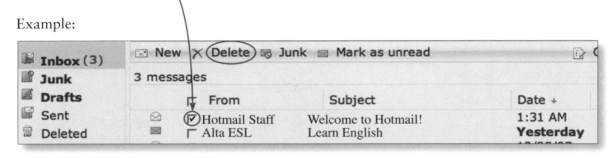.

2. Go to the Web site: www.hotmail.com.

3. Sign in to your email account.

4. Click **Inbox**.

5. Click one check box.

6. Click **Delete**.

Example:

Practice

1. Send an email to your partner.

2. Read an email.

3. Reply to an email.

4. Delete one email.

5. Click **Sign out**.

6. Disconnect from the Internet ⊠ .

11.15 My Portfolio: Five Keys to Good Health

Before You Start

Ask a neighbor or friend for five keys to good health. Write them here:

Five Keys to Good Health

1. _____

2. _____

3. _____

4. _____

5. _____

Five Keys to Good Health

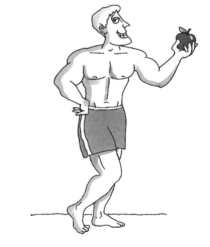

1. Open Microsoft Word [W].

2. Save the document as **yourname.11.15.keystogoodhealth** [💾].

3. Type a heading with your name, the date, and your teacher's name. Align it to the right [≣].

4. Use Word Art to insert the title **Five Keys to Good Health**.

5. Insert a footer with the file name and page numbers.

6. Type the five keys to good health.

7. Save [💾].

8. Print [🖨].

9. Add this page to your portfolio.

10. Close Microsoft Word [✖].

Example:

John Doe
June 2, 2092
Instructor: Tina Sander

Five Keys to Good Health

Walk every day.
Drink lots of water.
Sleep at least 8 hours every day.
Be nice to people.
Eat fruits and vegetables.

johndoe11.15.keystogoodhealth   Page 1 of 1

11.16 Homework

The Internet: A Hospital

1. Connect to the Internet .

2. Open the Web site: **www.google.com.**

3. Type the word **hospital**, your city, and your state/province.

4. Click **Google Search** .

5. Write the hospital's Web address:

   _____

6. Write the street address and phone number of the hospital:

Hospital

Street Address: _____

Phone number: _____

---

7. Disconnect from the Internet **✕** .

Email

1. Connect to the Internet .
2. Go to the Web site: **www.hotmail.com**.
3. Sign in to your email account.
4. You don't feel well. Send an email to a friend asking for advice.
5. Reply to an email.
6. Delete an email.
7. Click **Sign out**.
8. Disconnect from the Internet .

Example:

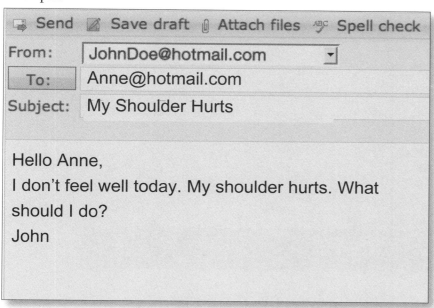

⊳ Send	✎ Save draft	📎 Attach files	ᴬᴮᶜ Spell check

From: JohnDoe@hotmail.com ▼

To: Anne@hotmail.com

Subject: My Shoulder Hurts

Hello Anne,
I don't feel well today. My shoulder hurts. What
should I do?
John

Unit 11 End-of-Unit Checklist

REVIEW		
I can . . .		
. . . insert footers in Microsoft Word documents.	☐ Yes!	☐ Not yet.
. . . use WordArt and Clip Art.	☐ Yes!	☐ Not yet.
. . . use the Start menu to connect to the Internet.	☐ Yes!	☐ Not yet.
. . . copy and paste images from the Internet.	☐ Yes!	☐ Not yet.
. . . use the Start menu to open Microsoft Word.	☐ Yes!	☐ Not yet.
. . . switch between the Internet and Microsoft Word.	☐ Yes!	☐ Not yet.
. . . send and reply to emails.	☐ Yes!	☐ Not yet.

UNIT 11		
I can . . .		
. . . insert borders in Microsoft Word documents.	☐ Yes!	☐ Not yet.
. . . copy and paste words from the Internet.	☐ Yes!	☐ Not yet.
. . . copy and paste Web addresses.	☐ Yes!	☐ Not yet.
. . . use the refresh button.	☐ Yes!	☐ Not yet.
. . . delete emails.	☐ Yes!	☐ Not yet.

What Do You Like to Do?

12.1 Vocabulary

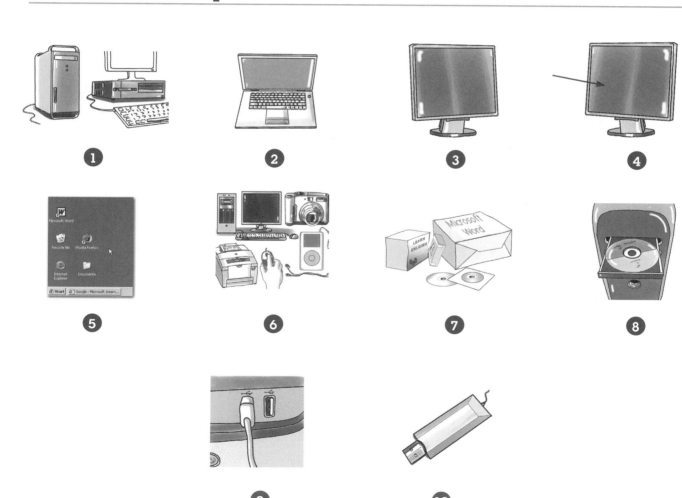

12.2 Speaking

PARTNER A: *Look at page 171.*

PARTNER B: *Look at page 172. Say the words.*

PARTNER A: *Point to the picture.*

Change roles and repeat.

1. desktop computer

2. laptop computer

3. monitor

4. screen

5. desktop

6. computer hardware

7. computer software (programs)

8. CD drive

9. USB port

10. memory stick

12.3 Writing

Listen to your teacher. Write the words. Show your partner.

1. _____

2. _____

3. _____

4. _____

5. _____

6. _____

7. _____

8. _____

9. _____

10. _____

> **!** **IMPORTANT . . .**
>
> **Try a new computer program:**
>
>

12.4 My Portfolio: My Free Time

Review

1. Open Microsoft Word.

2. Save the document as **yourname.12.4.freetime**.

3. Type a heading with your name, the date, and your teacher's name. Align it to the right.

4. Insert a footer with the file name and page numbers.

5. Use WordArt to type the title **My Free Time**. Center. Press **Enter** two times.

6. Type a paragraph about what you and your family do in your free time. Align the paragraph to the left. Indent the first word.

7. Insert a Clip Art picture of one activity:

   - Use the Start menu to connect to the Internet.

   - Open the Web site: **www.outandaboutenglish.com**.

   - Click **Unit 12**.

   - Click **Activities**.

   - Copy and paste an image from the Web page to your Microsoft Word document.

Example:

John Doe
February 11, 2075
Instructor: Tina Sander

My Free Time

I like to swim, play tennis, surf, and watch TV. My brother likes to play basketball. My mother likes to go hiking in the summer. My sister likes to read books and play volleyball. We all like to watch movies.

johndoe.12.4.freetime   Page 1 of 1

8. Copy and paste an image of one of your family's activities from www.google.com.

9. Insert a border:

- Click **Format.**
- Click **Borders and Shading.**
- Click **Page Border.**
- Click **Box.**
- Select **Art.**
- Click **OK.**

10. Save.

11. Print.

12. Add this page to your portfolio.

13. Close Microsoft Word.

14. Disconnect from the Internet.

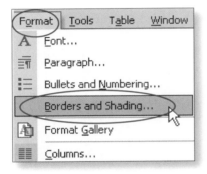

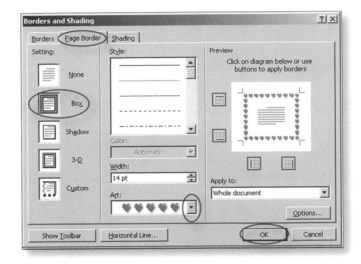

12.5 Microsoft Word: Page Setup

Orientation

1. Open Microsoft Word.

2. Open **yourname.12.4.freetime.**

3. Click **File.**

4. Click **Page Setup.**

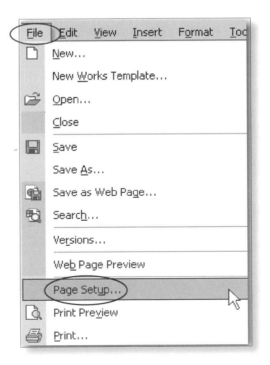

5. Click **Margins.**

6. Click **Landscape.**

7. Click **OK.**

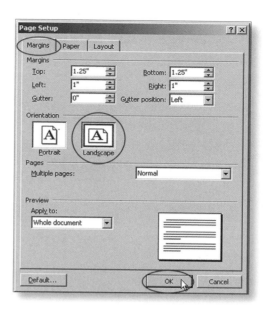

Margins

1. Continue working with the document **yourname.12.4.freetime.**

2. Click **File.**

3. Click **Page Setup.**

4. Click **Margins.**

5. Click  to change the number of inches. ——→ Top: 2"

Left: 1.5"   Right: 1.5"

6. Click **OK.**

7. Save.

8. Close Microsoft Word.

Bottom: 2"

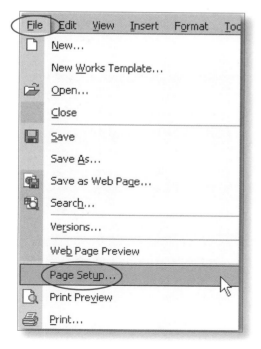

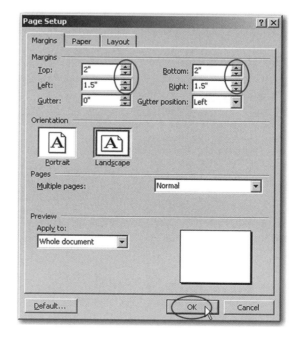

12.6 The Internet: Weather Around the World

1. Open Microsoft Word.

2. Save the document as **yourname.12.6.weather.**

3. Type a heading with your name, the date, and your teacher's name. Align it to the right.

4. Insert a footer with the file name and page numbers.

5. Change the orientation to **landscape:**
   - Click **File.**
   - Click **Page Setup.**
   - Click **Margins.**
   - Click **Landscape.**
   - Click **OK.**

6. Change all the margins to 1 inch:
   - Click **File.**
   - Click **Page Setup.**
   - Click **Margins.**
   - Click ⬔ to change the number of inches.
   - Click **OK.**

7. Insert a table with three rows and five columns.

8. Use the Start menu to connect to the Internet.

9. Open the Web site: **www.outandaboutenglish.com.**

10. Click **Unit 12.**

11. Click **The Weather.**

Top: 1"

Left: 1"   Right: 1"

Bottom: 1"

12. Copy and paste the city names into the first row of your Microsoft Word table.

13. Copy and paste the weather images into the second row of your Microsoft Word table.

14. In the third row of your table, type a weather word for each city.

Example:

Mexico City	Hamburg	Casablanca	Chicago	Nagano
☀				
Sunny				

15. Save.

16. Close Microsoft Word.

17. Disconnect from the Internet.

12.7 The Internet: Weather Reports

1. Connect to the Internet.
2. Open the Web site: www.outandaboutenglish.com.
3. Click **Unit 12.**
4. Click **Weather Reports.**
5. Write the answers:

A Weather Report

a. Where will it be sunny this week? _____

b. When will it rain in Portland? _____

c. Where will it snow? _____

d. Which city will be the coldest at night? _____

e. Which city will be the hottest during the day? _____

f. What kind of weather do you like? _____

---

6. Disconnect from the Internet.

12.8 My Portfolio: The Weather In My City

1. Open Microsoft Word.

2. Save the document as **yourname.12.8.weatherinmycity.**

3. Type a heading with your name, the date and your teacher's name. Align it to the right.

4. Insert a footer with the file name and page numbers.

5. Use WordArt to type the title **The Weather In My City.** Center. Press **Enter** two times.

6. Type a paragraph about the weather in your city. What is the weather in the spring, summer, fall, and winter? Align the paragraph to the left. Indent the first word.

7. Save.

8. Find this week's weather report for your city:

   • Connect to the Internet.

   • Open the Web site: www.yahoo.com.

   • Type **weather report,** the name of your city, and your state or province in the search box. Press **Enter.**

9. Read the weather report for this week.

10. Copy and paste the weather report from the Web page into your Microsoft Word document.

Example:

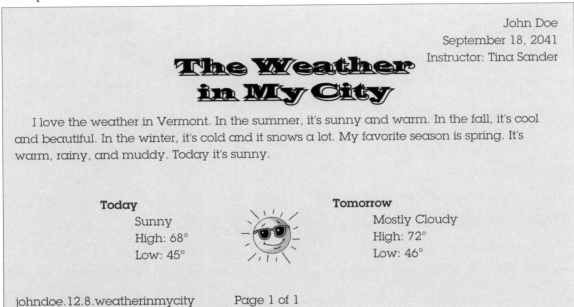

11. Save.

12. Print.

13. Add this page to your portfolio.

14. Close Microsoft Word.

12.9 The Internet: TV Listings

Before You Start

Ask your partner and write the answers:

Watching TV

a. Do you like to watch TV? _____

b. How often do you watch TV? _____

c. What is your favorite TV show? _____

d. Why do you like it? _____

TV Listings

1. Connect to the Internet.

2. Open the Web site: www.outandaboutenglish.com.

3. Click **Unit 12.**

4. Click **TV Listings.**

5. Read the TV listings.

6. Write the answers:

TV Listings

a. What are the channels? _____

_____

_____

b. What are the times? _____

_____

_____

c. List three TV programs: _____

_____

_____

d. List three movies: _____

_____

_____

e. List three
   sports programs: _____

_____

_____

---

7. Disconnect from the Internet.

12.10 Inserting a Table: TV Listings

1. Use the Start menu to open Microsoft Word.

2. Insert a table with six columns and six rows. Save.

3. Use the Start menu to connect to the Internet.

4. Open the Web site: www.tv.yahoo.com/listings.

5. Select times from the Web page. Type the times in the first row of your Microsoft Word table. Make them bold.

6. Select channels from the Web page. Type the channels in the first column of your table. Make them bold.

7. Type TV programs from the Web page in the other cells of your table.

8. Save.

9. Share your listing with your partner.

Example:

	5:00	5:30	6:00	6:30	7:00
Channel 3	Baseball	Police Story	News	Twin Peaks	Love Boat
Channel 9	Author's Chair	Cartoons	News	News	Hiking Today
Channel 34	Movie: Bambi	Movie: Bambi	Cooking	Soccer	Soccer
Channel 48	Evening Magazine	Columbo	E.R.	Movie: The Women	Movie: The Women
Channel 72	Basketball	Basketball	Movie: Cats	Movie: Cats	Movie: Cats

10. Close Microsoft Word.

11. Disconnect from the Internet.

12.11 The Internet: Movie Listings

Before You Start

Ask your partner and write the answers:

Movies

a. Do you like movies? _____

b. What kinds of movies do you watch? _____

c. What is your favorite movie? _____

d. What movie do you want to see? _____

Decide who is Partner A and who is Partner B.

Movie Listings

Partner A

Ask your partner for the missing information:

Scotts Valley Cinema	
Street Address: _____	
The Explorer Rated R, 1 hr 42 min **Showtimes:** _____	**Movie Title:** _____ Rated PG, ____ hr ____ min **Showtimes:** (12:00), (12:40), (2:10), (2:50), (4:30), (5:00), 6:45, 7:15, 8:50, 9:20, 10:50
Over the Rainbow Rated R, 2 hr 9 min **Showtimes:** _____	**Girls Rule** Not Rated, 1 hr 46 min **Showtimes:** _____

Partner B

1. Connect to the Internet.

2. Open the Web site: www.outandaboutenglish.com.

3. Click **Unit 12**.

4. Click **Movie Listings**.

5. Click **Partner B** .

6. Answer your partner's questions.

7. Disconnect from the Internet.

Movie Listings

Partner B

Ask your partner for the missing information:

Nickelodeon Theater	
Street Address: _____	
Running on Zero	**In Our Lifetime**
Rated R, 1 hr 40 min	*Rated PG, 1 hr 30 min*
Showtimes: _____	**Showtimes:** _____
Movie Title: _____	**Family Fun**
Rated R, 2 hr 9 min	*Not Rated, ____ hr ____ min*
Showtimes: (1:05), 4:00, 6:55, 9:45	**Showtimes:** (12:15), (2:35), 4:50, 7:05, 9:20

Partner A

1. Connect to the Internet.

2. Open the Web site: www.outandaboutenglish.com.

3. Click **Unit 12**.

4. Click **Movie Listings**.

5. Click   Partner A   .

6. Answer your partner's questions.

7. Disconnect from the Internet.

12.12 The Internet: Movies in Your Neighborhood

1. Connect to the Internet.

2. Open the Web site: www.yahoo.com.

3. Click **Movies**.

4. Type your zip code in the **Browse by Location** text box.

5. Click **Go**.

6. Answer the questions:

Watching Movies

a. What movie do you want to see? _____

b. What theater do you want to go to? _____

c. What time is the movie showing? _____

d. What is the theater's address? _____

---

7. Show your partner.

8. Disconnect from the Internet.

12.13 Email: Review

Using Email

1. Connect to the Internet.

2. Open the Web site: www.hotmail.com.

3. Sign in to your email account.

4. Type an email to your partner:
   What did you do this weekend?

5. Click **Send**.

6. Read your partner's email.

7. Reply to your partner's email.

8. Delete an email.

9. Click **Sign out**.

10. Disconnect from the Internet.

Example:

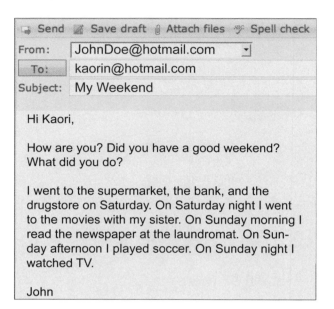

12.14 Email: Saving Email Addresses

1. Connect to the Internet.

2. Open the Web site: www.hotmail.com.

3. Sign in to your email account.

4. Type an email to your partner.

5. Click **Send**.

6. Save your partner's email address:
   - Type your partner's first name in the **First name** text box.
   - Type your partner's last name in the **Last Name** text box.
   - Click **Add to contacts**.
   - Click **Contacts**. Do you see your partner's name and email address? _____

7. Click **Sign out**.

8. Disconnect from the Internet.

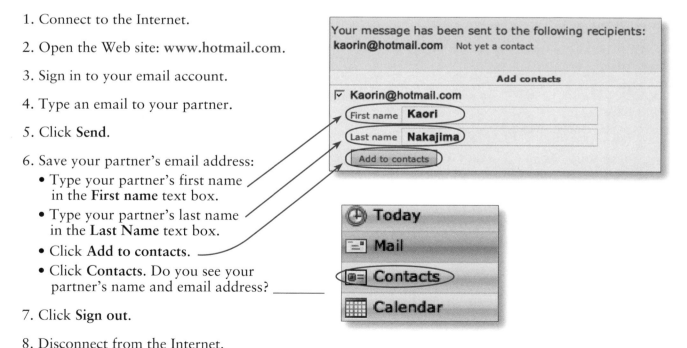

Note to the Teacher: Hotmail instructions adhere to use of the Classic version of Hotmail. See the online teacher's guide at www.outandaboutenglish.com for more information.

12.15 Email: Sending Emails to Saved Email Addresses

1. Connect to the Internet.

2. Open the Web site: www.hotmail.com.

3. Sign in to your email account.

4. Click ▣ **New** .

5. Click on ⬚ To: ⬚ .

6. Check the box for your partner's name.

7. Click **Add contacts to message.**

8. Type **My Free Time** in the subject line.

9. Type an email to your partner: What do you do in your free time?

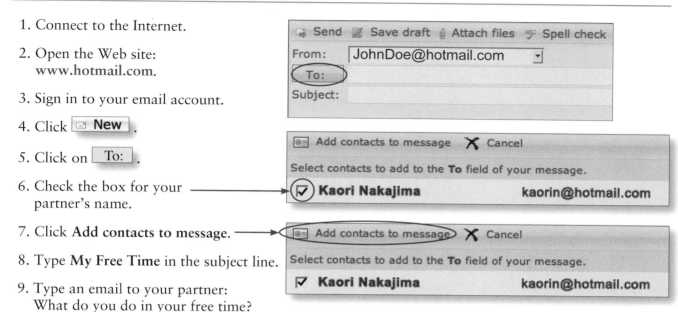

Example:

10. Click **Send.**

11. Click **Sign out.**

12. Disconnect from the Internet.

12.16 My Portfolio: My Contacts List

1. Open Microsoft Word.

2. Save the document as **yourname.12.16.contactslist.**

3. Type a heading with your name, the date, and your teacher's name. Align it to the right.

4. Insert a footer with the file name and page numbers.

5. Insert a table with five columns and five rows.

6. Type **Name, Relation, Address, Phone Number,** and **Email Address** in the first row. Bold the words.

7. Type your partner's name, relation, address, and phone number in the second row.

8. Save.

9. Connect to the Internet.

10. Open the Web site: **www.hotmail.com.**

11. Sign in to your email account.

12. Click **Contacts.**

13. Copy your partner's email address:
    - Highlight an email address.
    - Right click.
    - Click **Copy.**

14. Switch to Microsoft Word.

15. Paste your partner's email address into the last cell:
    - Right click in the cell.
    - Left click **Paste.**

16. Save.

17. Close Microsoft Word.

18. Sign out of your email account.

19. Disconnect from the Internet.

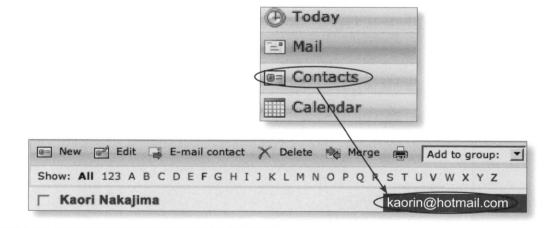

Example:

Name	Relation	Address	Phone Number	Email Address
Kaori Nakajima	Friend	524 Main Street	555-567-0929	kaorin@hotmail.com

12.17 My Portfolio: Famous Places

Before You Start

1. Choose a country: _____

2. Write three famous places in the country:

Famous Places

a. _____

b. _____

c. _____

3. Connect to the Internet. Open the Web site: **www.google.com**.

4. Search for the three famous places. Find a Web address for each famous place. Write the addresses:

Web Addresses

a. _____

b. _____

c. _____

5. Disconnect from the Internet.

Famous Places

1. Open Microsoft Word.

2. Save the document as **yourname.12.17.famousplaces**.

3. Type a heading with your name, the date, and your teacher's name. Align it to the right.

4. Type a title using WordArt.

5. Insert a footer with the file name and page numbers.

6. Insert a table with four rows and two columns.

7. Type **Web Addresses** and **Famous Places** in the first row. Bold the words.

8. Type the three Web addresses of the famous places from page 187 in the left column.

9. Type the names of the famous places in the right column.

10. Connect to the Internet.

11. Open the Web site: **www.google.com**.

12. Search for images of the three famous places.

13. Copy and paste an image of each place in the right column of your table.

14. Add a border to your document.

15. Change the margins to .5 inches.

16. Save.

17. Print.

18. Add this page to your portfolio.

19. Close Microsoft Word.

20. Disconnect from the Internet.

Example:

John Doe
October 12, 2051
Instructor: Tina Sander

The USA

Web Addresses	Famous Places
www.statueofliberty.org	The Statue of Liberty
www.goldengatebridge.org	The Golden Gate Bridge
www.nps.gov/grca	The Grand Canyon

johndoe.12.17.famousplaces   Page 1 of 1

12.18 Homework

Using Email

1. Connect to the Internet.

2. Go to the Web site: www.hotmail.com.

3. Sign in to your email account.

4. Click 🖃 **New** .

5. Type an email to a friend about your three famous places from **activity 12.17**.

6. Click **Send.**

7. Save your friend's email address:
   • Type your friend's first name in the **First name** text box.
   • Type your friend's last name in the **Last name** text box.
   • Click **Add to contacts.**

8. Send one email to a saved address:
   • Click 🖃 **New** .
   • Click on **To:** .
   • Check the box of the person you want to email.
   • Click **Add contacts to message.**
   • Type and send an email.

9. Reply to an email.

10. Delete an email.

11. Click **Sign out.**

Example:

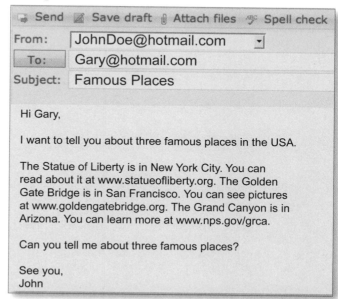

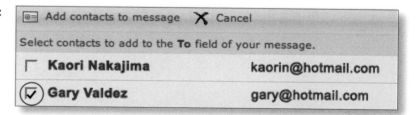

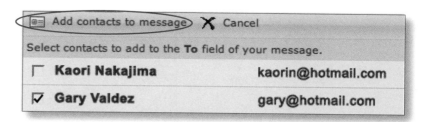

Unit 12 End-of-Unit Checklist

REVIEW		
I can . . .		
. . . insert footers in Microsoft Word documents.	☐ Yes!	☐ Not yet.
. . . use WordArt and Clip Art.	☐ Yes!	☐ Not yet.
. . . switch between the Internet and Microsoft Word.	☐ Yes!	☐ Not yet.
. . . copy and paste images from the Internet.	☐ Yes!	☐ Not yet.
. . . insert borders in Microsoft Word documents.	☐ Yes!	☐ Not yet.
. . . send, read, reply, and delete emails.	☐ Yes!	☐ Not yet.
UNIT 12		
I can . . .		
. . . change the orientation of Microsoft Word documents.	☐ Yes!	☐ Not yet.
. . . change the margins on Microsoft Word documents.	☐ Yes!	☐ Not yet.
. . . use www.yahoo.com to find information.	☐ Yes!	☐ Not yet.
. . . save email addresses.	☐ Yes!	☐ Not yet.
. . . send emails to saved email addresses.	☐ Yes!	☐ Not yet.
. . . copy and paste email addresses.	☐ Yes!	☐ Not yet.

How Do You Get to School?

13.1 Vocabulary

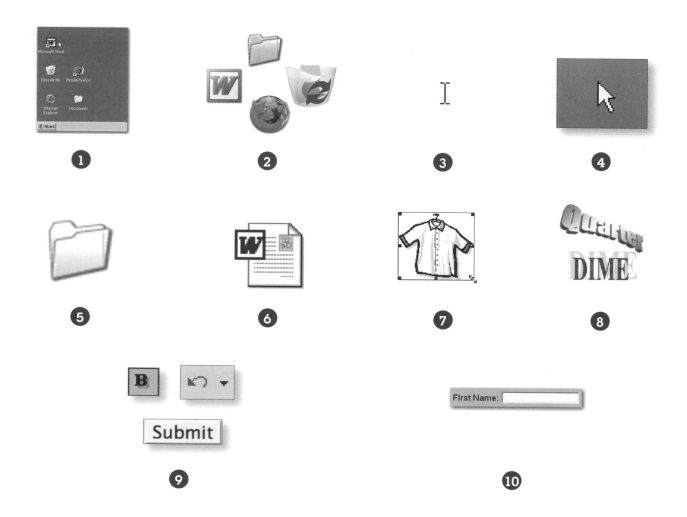

13.2 Speaking

PARTNER A: *Look at page 191.*

PARTNER B: *Look at page 192. Say the words.*

PARTNER A: *Point to the picture.*

Change roles and repeat.

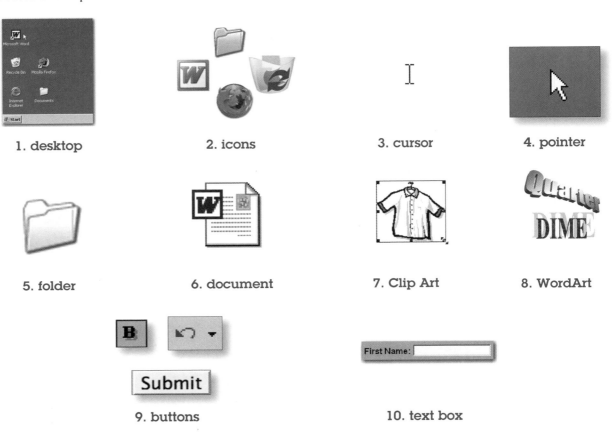

1. desktop   2. icons   3. cursor   4. pointer

5. folder   6. document   7. Clip Art   8. WordArt

9. buttons   10. text box

13.3 Writing

Listen to your teacher. Write the words. Show your partner.

1. _____   6. _____

2. _____   7. _____

3. _____   8. _____

4. _____   9. _____

5. _____   10. _____

IMPORTANT . . .

Bring something new to class . . .

cell phone   digital camera   mP3 player (iPod)   PDA

13.4 My Portfolio: Transportation

Review

1. Open Microsoft Word.
2. Save the document as **yourname.13.4.transportation**.
3. Type a heading with your name, the date, and your teacher's name. Align it to the right.
4. Insert a footer with the file name and page numbers.
5. Use WordArt to type the title: **Transportation**. Center. Press **Enter**.
6. Change the orientation to landscape:
   - Click **File**.
   - Click **Page Setup**.
   - Click **Margins**.
   - Click **Landscape**.
   - Click **OK**.

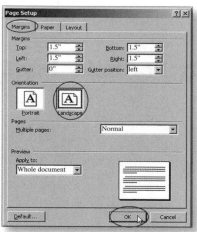

7. Change the margins:
   - Click **File**.
   - Click **Page Setup**.
   - Click **Margins**.
   - Change all the margins to **1.5"**.
   - Click **OK**.

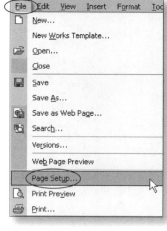
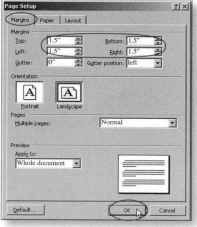

8. Insert a table with eight columns and two rows.

9. Type in the first row: **By Bus, By Bicycle, By Motorcycle, By Car, By Subway, By Train, By Taxi,** and **On Foot**. Bold the words.

10. Use the Start menu to connect to the Internet.

11. Open the Web site: **www.outandaboutenglish.com**.

12. Click **Unit 13**.

13. Click **Transportation**.

14. Copy and paste eight matching images from the Internet into your table.

Example:

15. Save.

16. Print.

17. Add this page to your portfolio.

18. Close Microsoft Word.

19. Disconnect from the Internet.

John Doe
May 23, 2024
Instructor: Tina Sander

Transportation

By Bus	By Bicycle	By Motorcycle	By Car	By Subway	By Train	By Taxi	On Foot
🚌	🚲						

johndoe.13.4.transportation   Page 1 of 1

13.5 My Portfolio: My Computer Skills

1. Open Microsoft Word.

2. Save your document as **yourname.13.5.computerskills**.

3. Type a heading with your name, the date, and your teacher's name. Align it to the right.

4. Insert a footer with the file name and page numbers.

5. Use WordArt to type the title: **My Computer Skills**. Center. Press **Enter**.

6. Type and bold **Microsoft Word**. Align it to the left.

7. Type a list of your Microsoft Word skills.

8. Type and bold **The Internet**.

9. Type a list of your Internet skills.

10. Type and bold **Email**.

11. Type a list of your email skills.

12. Copy and paste an image from the Internet:

- Use the Start menu to connect to the Internet.
- Open the Web site: **www.outandaboutenglish.com**.
- Click **Unit 13**.
- Click **Computer Images**.
- Copy an image.
- Switch to Microsoft Word.
- Paste the image.

13. Add a border to your document.

14. Save.

15. Print.

16. Add this page to your portfolio.

17. Close Microsoft Word.

18. Disconnect from the Internet.

Example:

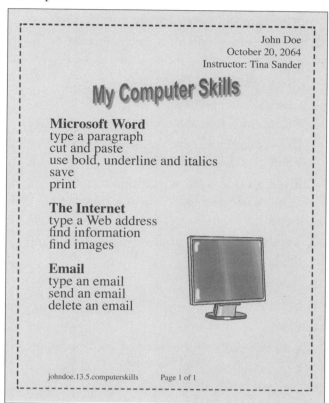

John Doe
October 20, 2064
Instructor: Tina Sander

My Computer Skills

Microsoft Word
type a paragraph
cut and paste
use bold, underline and italics
save
print

The Internet
type a Web address
find information
find images

Email
type an email
send an email
delete an email

johndoe.13.5.computerskills   Page 1 of 1

13.6 My Portfolio: Table of Contents

Before You Start

Look at the table of contents in this book. Answer the questions:

Table of Contents

a. Where are the page numbers? _____

b. How many units are in the book? _____

c. What is the name of the first unit? _____

Table of Contents

1. Count all the portfolio pages you have printed. How many do you have? _____

2. Number your portfolio pages. Put the cover page first.

3. Open Microsoft Word.

4. Save the document as **yourname.13.6.tableofcontents**.

5. Use WordArt to type the title **Table of Contents**. Center.

6. Insert a table with two columns and the number of rows equal to your number of portfolio pages (step 1).

7. Type the names of your portfolio pages and the page numbers.

8. Add a border.

9. Save.

10. Print.

11. Add this page to the front of your portfolio.

12. Close Microsoft Word.

Example:

Table of Contents

My Weekly Schedule	2
A Birthday Calendar	3
My Contact Information	4
My Family	5
My Partner's Family	6
Famous People	7
My Home Activities	8
My Favorite Recipe	9
About Me	10
A Party Invitation	11
A Restaurant Advertisement	12
My Home	13
My Community	14
My Native Country	15
My Community Contacts	16
Body Parts	17
Five Keys to Good Health	18
My Free Time	19
The Weather in My City	20
My Contacts List	21
Transportation	22
Famous Places	23
My Computer Skills	24
My Favorite Web Sites	25

Note to the Teacher: The last portfolio page in this example is completed later in this unit.

13.7 Deleting a Microsoft Word Document

1. Create a document:
   - Open Microsoft Word.
   - Save the document as **yourname.13.7.delete1**.

2. Close Microsoft Word.

3. Open Microsoft Word.

4. Click **File**.

5. Click **Open**.

6. Right click **yourname.13.7.delete1**.

7. Select **Delete**.

8. Click **Yes**.

9. Repeat steps 1-8 with **yourname.13.7.delete2**.

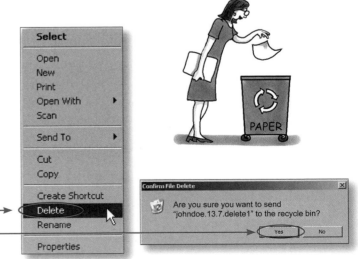

13.8 The Internet: Searching for Maps

Before You Start

What's your home address?

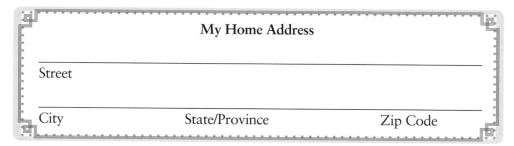

My Home Address

_____

Street

_____

City   State/Province   Zip Code

Searching for Maps 1

1. Find a map of your neighborhood:
   - Connect to the Internet.
   - Open the Web site: www.google.com.
   - Click Maps .
   - Type your home address in the text box.
   - Click Search Maps .
   - Look at the map.
   - Show your partner.

Before You Start

What's your school address?

My School Address

_____

Street

_____

City   State/Province   Zip Code

Searching for Maps 2

1. Find a map of your school using the Web site: www.google.com.

2. Look at your map with a partner.

3. Write the names of three streets that you see:

   1. _____

   2. _____

   3. _____

13.9 The Internet: Searching for Directions

Before You Start

How do you get from your home to school? Write the directions.

Example: I come to school by car. I live on Oak Street. I leave my house and turn right on Oak Street. I go straight for two blocks and turn left on Canyon Avenue. I go straight for four miles and turn left on Madrone Lane. I continue for one mile and then turn right into the school parking lot.

Directions

_____

_____

_____

_____

_____

Searching for Directions

1. Connect to the Internet.

2. Open the Web site: **www.google.com**.

3. Click Maps .

4. Click **Get directions**.

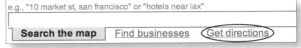

5. Type your home address in the **Start address** text box.

6. Type your school address in the **End address** text box.

7. Click Get Directions .

8. Read the directions and answer these questions:

a. How long does it take to drive from your home to school? _____

b. How many miles is it from your home to school? _____

c. Are the directions correct? _____

9. Disconnect from the Internet.

13.10 The Internet: A Bus Schedule

Before You Start

Ask your partner the questions. Write the answers. Use the vocabulary to help you.

1. How do you get to school? _____

2. How do you get to work? _____

3. Do you ever take the train? _____ How often? _____

4. Do you ever take the subway? _____ How often? _____

5. Do you ever take the bus? _____ How often? _____

6. Do you ever travel by airplane? _____ How often? _____

every day	sometimes	once a week
twice a month	three times a year	
occasionally	rarely	never

A Bus Schedule

1. Connect to the Internet.
2. Open the Web site: www.outandaboutenglish.com.
3. Click **Unit 13**.
4. Click **Bus Schedule**.
5. Read the schedule. Write the answers:

A Bus Schedule

a. What time does the first bus leave North Station? _____

b. Where does the bus go? _____

_____

c. How long does it take to go from North Station to South Station? _____

d. What is the bus route number? _____

e. Does this bus run every day? _____

f. What days does this bus run? _____

---

6. Check your answers with a partner.
7. Disconnect from the Internet.

13.11 The Internet: Searching for a Bus Schedule

1. Connect to the Internet.
2. Open the Web site: www.google.com.
3. Type **Bus Schedule,** the name of your city, and your state or province.
4. Click ⬚ Google Search ⬚ .
5. Find a bus schedule. Write the Web address: _____
6. Write the information:

Bus Line	Start Location	Start Time	End Location	End Time

7. Disconnect from the Internet.

13.12 The Internet: An Airline Schedule

Before You Start

Ask your partner the questions. Write the answers:

Traveling By Airplane

a. When was the last time you traveled by airplane? _____

b. Where did you go? _____

c. How long did it take? _____

d. Where do you want to fly in the future? _____

e. When do you want to go there? _____

An Airline Schedule

1. Connect to the Internet.

2. Open the Web site: www.outandaboutenglish.com.

3. Click **Unit 13**.

4. Click **An Airline Schedule**.

5. Answer these questions:

> ### An Airline Schedule
>
> a. What's the airline company? _____
>
> b. How many flights are there to Boston? _____
>
> c. How many flights are there to San Francisco? _____
>
> d. Which flights are non-stop? _____
>
> e. What is another word for schedule? _____
>
> f. How many itineraries are there? _____

6. Write the information:

San Francisco, CA (SFO) to Boston, MA (BOS)	Itinerary #1	Itinerary #2
How much does the ticket cost?	$698.40	
How long does the flight take?		
Is it non-stop?		
Is it a morning, afternoon, evening, or night flight?		

7. Which itinerary do you like? _____

8. Why do you like this itinerary? _____

9. Disconnect from the Internet.

13.13 The Internet: Finding a Flight

Before You Start

Ask your teacher for a travel Web site. Write the Web address:

_____

Where do you want to go?

> **I want to go . . .**
>
> From (City): _____   To (City): _____

Finding a Flight

1. Connect to the Internet.

2. Open the travel Web site.

3. Find a roundtrip flight.

4. Write the information in the table:

Airline	Flight Number	Date	Departure Time	Arrival Time	Stops

5. What is the total cost of this flight? _____

6. Disconnect from the Internet.

Example:

Airline	Flight Number	Date	Departure Time	Arrival Time	Stops
United	1185	Feb. 1, 2117	8:00 am	2:45 pm	1
United	2047	Feb. 9, 2117	6:30 pm	11:45 pm	0

Note to the Teacher: See the online teacher's guide at www.outandaboutenglish.com for suggested travel Web sites.

13.14 Web Sites for Learning English

Internet Search

1. Connect to the Internet.

2. Open the Web site: www.google.com.

3. Search for a Web site for learning English.

4. Write the Web address:

_____

5. Click on the word and image links.

6. What can you practice? Circle one or more:

| grammar | vocabulary | spelling | reading | listening | writing |

Email

7. Open the Web site: www.hotmail.com.

8. Sign in to your email account.

9. Click **Inbox**.

10. Click **New**.

11. Send an email to your partner:

    • Copy and paste the Web address for learning English.

    • Type a message about the Web site.

    • Click **Send**.

12. Click **Sign out**.

13. Disconnect from the Internet.

Example:

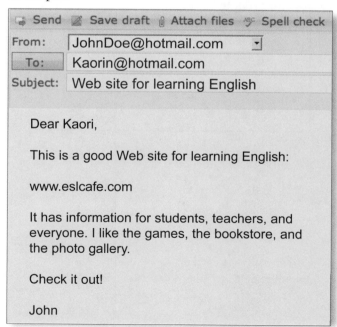

Note to the Teacher: See the online teacher's guide at www.outandaboutenglish.com for suggested Web sites for learning English.

13.15 My Portfolio: My Favorite Web Sites

1. Open Microsoft Word.

2. Save the document as **yourname.13.15.myfavoritewebsites.**

3. Type a heading with your name, the date, and your teacher's name. Align it to the right.

4. Insert a footer with the file name and page numbers.

5. Use WordArt to type the title: **My Favorite Web Sites.** Center.

6. Change the orientation to **landscape.**

7. Change all the margins to **1.5".**

8. Insert a table with three columns and four rows.

9. Type in the first row: **Web Site, Information,** and **Picture.** Bold the words.

Example:

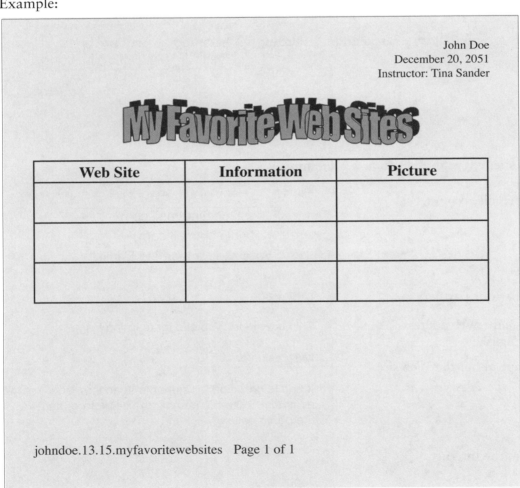

Note to the Teacher: This portfolio page will need to be added to the Table of Contents document done in 13.6.

10. Use the Start menu to connect to the Internet.

11. Go to the Web site: www.google.com.

12. Find three favorite Web sites.

13. Copy and paste the Web addresses into the **Web Site** column of your Microsoft Word table.

14. Type information about each Web address into the **Information** column.

15. Copy and paste images from the Web sites into the **Picture** column.

16. Add a border.

17. Save.

18. Print.

19. Add this page to your portfolio.

20. Close Microsoft Word.

21. Disconnect from the Internet.

Example:

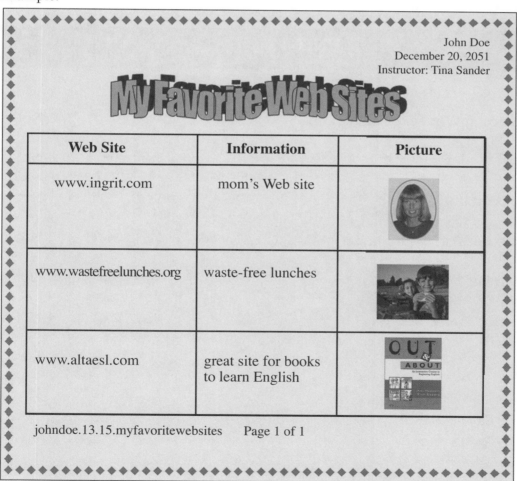

Unit 13 End-of-Unit Checklist

REVIEW		
I can . . .		
. . . change the orientation of Microsoft Word documents.	☐ Yes!	☐ Not yet.
. . . change the margins in Microsoft Word documents.	☐ Yes!	☐ Not yet.
. . . switch between the Internet and Microsoft Word.	☐ Yes!	☐ Not yet
. . . copy and paste images from the Internet.	☐ Yes!	☐ Not yet.
UNIT 13		
I can . . .		
. . . delete a Microsoft Word document.	☐ Yes!	☐ Not yet.
. . . find maps on the Internet.	☐ Yes!	☐ Not yet.
. . . get directions on the Internet.	☐ Yes!	☐ Not yet.
. . . find bus schedules on the Internet.	☐ Yes!	☐ Not yet.
. . . find airline flights on the Internet.	☐ Yes!	☐ Not yet.
. . . practice English on the Internet.	☐ Yes!	☐ Not yet.

Unit 1

Turning on a Computer
page 4

- Turn on the computer.
- Turn on the monitor.
- Wait.

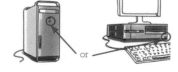

Turning off a Computer
page 4

- Click **Start**.
- Select **Turn Off Computer**.
- Click **Turn Off**.

Opening and Closing Microsoft Word
page 6

- To open, double-click ![W].
- To close, click ![X].

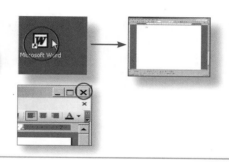

Unit 2

Saving a Microsoft Word Document
page 16

- Open Microsoft Word ![W].
- Click **File**.
- Click **Save** ![save].
- Click **My Documents**.
- Type the file name.
- Click **Save** ![save].

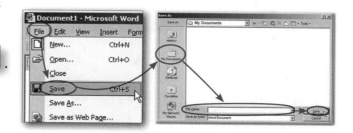

Opening a Microsoft Word Document
page 18

- Open Microsoft Word ![W].
- Click **File**.
- Click **Open** ![open].
- Click **My Documents**.
- Click your document.
- Click **Open**.

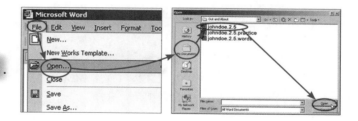

207

Unit 2 (continued)

Using the Undo Button and the Redo Button
page 20

- To undo, click ⟲ ▾ .
- To redo, click ▾ ⟳ .

Unit 3

Highlighting
page 28

- Click before the word.
- Hold down and move to the end of the word.
- Let go.

Typing: Bold
page 29

- Highlight the word.
- Click **B** .
- Click on white space.

Inserting Tables
page 31

- Click **Table**.
- Click **Insert**.
- Click **Table**.
- Type the **Number of columns**.
- Type the **Number of rows**.
- Click **OK**.

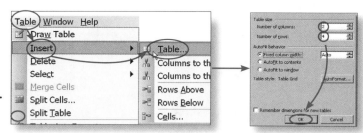

Using Print Preview
page 33

- Click **File**.
- Click **Print Preview** 🔍 .
- Look. Is the document OK?
- Click **Close**.

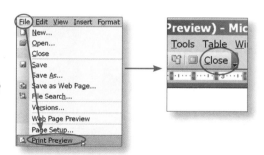

Unit 3 (continued)

Printing
page 34
- Click **File**.
- Click **Print**...
- Click OK.

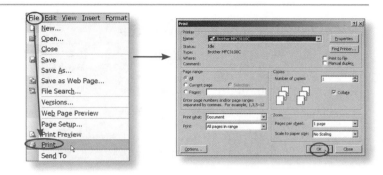

Unit 4

Typing: Italics
page 43
- Highlight the word.
- Click I.
- Click on white space.

Jobs → **Jobs** → *I* → *Jobs*

Typing: Underline
page 44
- Highlight the word.
- Click **U**.
- Click on white space.

Jobs → **Jobs** → **U** → <u>Jobs</u>

Opening a New Microsoft Word Document
page 44
- Open Microsoft Word.
- Open a document.
- Click.

Unit 5

Typing: Changing Colors
page 56
- Highlight the word.
- Click **A** ▼.
- Click a colored square.
- Click on white space.

Unit 5 (continued)

Typing: Making Words Bigger and Smaller
page 57

- Highlight the word.
- Click 12 ▾.
- Click on a size.
- Click on white space.

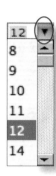

Unit 6

Typing: Changing Fonts
page 72

- Highlight the word.
- Click Times New Roman ▾.
- Click another font.
- Click on white space.

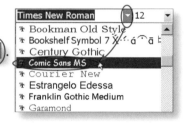

Cutting and Pasting
pages 72–73

To cut:

- Highlight the word.
- Click **Edit**.
- Click **Cut**.

To paste:

- Move the cursor.
- Click **Edit**.
- Click **Paste**.

Unit 7

Copying and Pasting
page 87

To copy:

- Highlight the word.
- Click **Edit**.
- Click **Copy**.

To paste:

- Move the cursor.
- Click **Edit**.
- Click **Paste**.

Unit 7 (continued)

Centering Words
page 91
- Highlight the words.
- Click 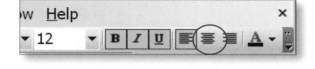.

Aligning Words to the Right
page 91
- Highlight the words.
- Click .

Aligning Words to the Left
page 93
- Highlight the words.
- Click .

Unit 8

Inserting WordArt
page 105
- Click **Insert**.
- Click **Picture**.
- Click **WordArt**.
- Click on a style.
- Click **OK**.
- Type the words.
- Click **OK**.

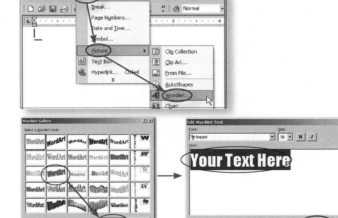

Resizing WordArt
page 106
- Click on the WordArt.
- Click and move a corner of the box.
- Click on white space.

Unit 9

Inserting Clip Art
page 120

- Position the cursor.
- Click **Insert**.
- Click **Picture**.
- Click **Clip Art**.
- Type the name of the image in the search text box.
- Click **Search**.
- Double-click a picture to insert.

Resizing ClipArt
page 120

- Click on the picture.
- Click and move a corner of the picture.

Unit 10

Inserting Footers
page 139

Insert a footer:
- Click **View**.
- Click **Header and Footer**.
- Click ▣ .

Insert the file name:
- Click **Insert AutoText**.
- Click **Filename**.
- Press **Tab**.

Insert page numbers:
- Click **Insert Auto Text**.
- Click **Page X of Y**.
- Click **Close**.

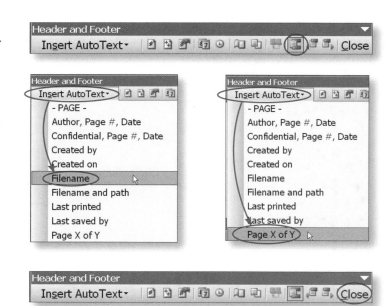

Unit 11

Inserting Borders
page 156

- Click **Format.**
- Click **Borders and Shading.**
- Click **Page Border.**
- Click **Box.**
- Select **Art** ▼ .
- Click **OK.**

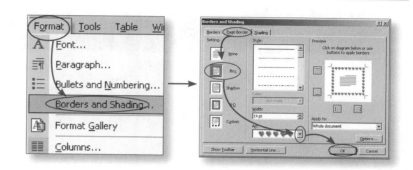

Unit 12

Microsoft Word: Page Setup
pages 174–175

To change page orientation:

- Click **File.**
- Click **Page Setup.**
- Click **Landscape** or **Portrait.**
- Click **OK.**

To change margins:

- Click **File.**
- Click **Page Setup.**
- Click **Margins.**
- Click ⬍ to change the number of inches.
- Click **OK.**

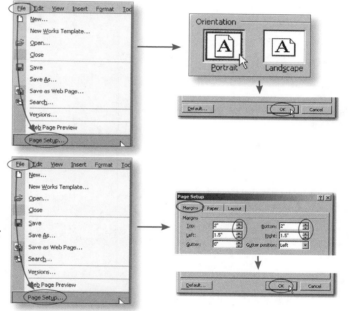

Unit 13

Deleting a Microsoft Word Document
page 196

- Click **File.**
- Click **Open.**
- Right click the document.
- Select **Delete.**
- Click **Yes.**

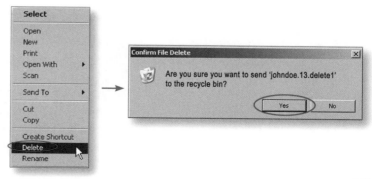

File name	Where is it?	Date

Unit 4

Connecting to and Disconnecting from the Internet
page 47

To connect:
- On your desktop, double-click .

To disconnect:
- Click .

Opening a Web Site
page 48
- Connect to the Internet .
- Click in the address field.
- Press **Backspace** to erase.
- Type the Web address.
- Press **Enter**.

Scrolling Up and Down in a Web Page
page 49

- Click to scroll down.
- Click to scroll up.

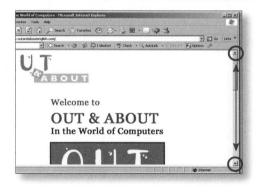

Unit 5

Using the Back Button
page 63

- Click on a link.
- Click Back .

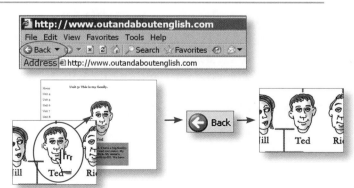

Unit 5 *(continued)*

Searching for Images
page 64

- Connect to the Internet 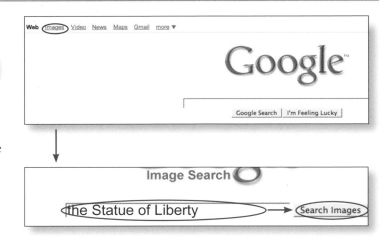.
- Open the Web site: www.google.com.
- Click Images .
- Type the name of the image in the search text box.
- Click Search Images .
- Click an image.

Unit 7

Using Drop-down Boxes
page 95

- Click ▼.
- Click the answer.

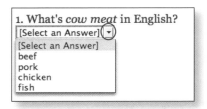

Using Radio Buttons
page 97

- Click yes no .

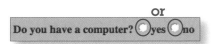

Unit 8

Searching the Internet
page 108

- Connect to the Internet .
- Open the Web site: www.google.com.
- Type the information in the search text box.
- Click Google Search .
- Click a link.

Unit 8 (continued)

Using Check Boxes
page 109
- Click the check boxes to answer the questions.

Using Text Boxes
page 109
- Click in the text box.
- Type the information.

Unit 10

Copying and Pasting Images
page 141

Copy an image from the Web page:
- Right click an image.
- Left click **Copy**.

Paste the image into Microsoft Word:
- Click  johndoe.10.4.myco... .
- Right click in the document.
- Left click **Paste**.
- Click on white space.

Unit 11

The Refresh Button
page 165

- Connect to the Internet.
- Open a Web site.
- Click Refresh.

Unit 11 (continued)

Copying and Pasting Web Addresses
page 164

- Highlight the Web address.
- Right click.
- Left click Copy.
- Open Microsoft Word 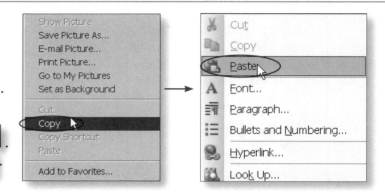.
- Open your document.
- Right click.
- Click Paste.
- Save.

Unit 13

Searching for Maps and Directions
page 197

- Connect to the Internet.
- Open the Web site: **www.google.com**.
- Click Maps.
- Type an address in the search text box.
- Click Search Maps.
- Read the map and directions.

Web Address	What is it?	Date

My Email Information

My Email Address: _____

My Password: _____

Unit 9

Signing In to and Out of Your Email Account
page 128
- Open the Web site: **www.hotmail.com**.
- Type your email address in the text box.
- Type your password in the text box.
- Click **Sign in**.
- Click **Sign out**.

Reading Emails
page 129
- Sign in to your email account.
- Click **Inbox**.
- Click an email.
- Read the message.
- Click **Sign out**.

Sending Emails
page 130
- Sign in to your email account.
- Click .
- In the **To** text box, type an email address.
- Type a subject in the **Subject** text box.
- In the **big text box,** type a message.
- Click **Send**.
- Click **Sign out**.

Unit 10

Replying to Emails
page 149

- Sign in to your email account.
- Open and read an email from your partner.
- Click **Reply**.
- Type a message.
- Click **Send**.
- Click **Sign out**.

Unit 11

Deleting Emails
page 166

- Sign in to your email account.
- Click **Inbox**.
- Click one check box.
- Click **Delete**.
- Click **Sign out**.

Unit 12

Saving Email Addresses
page 184

- Sign in to your email account.
- Click ✉ **New** .
- Type a message.
- Click **Send**.
- Type your contact's first name in the **First name** text box.
- Type your contact's last name in the **Last Name** text box.
- Click **Add to contacts**.
- Click **Sign out**.

Unit 12 (continued)

Sending Emails to Saved Email Addresses
page 185

- Sign in to your email account.
- Click ▣ **New** .
- Click on **To:** .
- Check the box(es) for the person(s) you want to send an email to.
- Click **Add contacts to message.**
- Type an email.
- Click **Send.**
- Click **Sign out.**

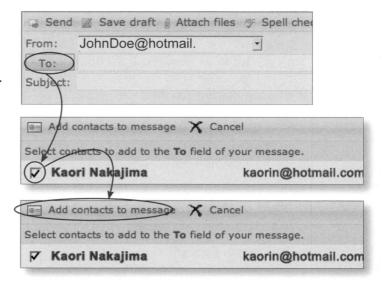